Allyn and Bacon

Quick Guide to the Internet for Speech-Language Pathology and Audiology

2000 Edition

Linda H. Leeper
New Mexico State University

Doug Gotthoffer
California State University–Northridge

Allyn and Bacon
Boston • London • Toronto • Sydney • Tokyo • Singapore

Executive Editor and Publisher: Steve Dragin
Multimedia Developmental Editor: Nina Tisch
Editorial Production: Marla Feuerstein
Cover Designer: Jennifer Hart
Editorial Production Service: Omegatype Typography, Inc.

ISBN 0-205-30970-4

Printed in the United States of America

10 9 8 7 6 5 4 3 2 02 01 00 99

Contents

Part 1 Introduction to the Internet

Part 2 Internet Activities for Speech-Language Pathology and Audiology

part 1

Introduction to the Internet

You're about to embark on an exciting experience as you become one of the millions of citizens of the Internet. In spite of what you might have heard, the Internet can be mastered by ordinary people before they earn a college degree and even if they're not majoring in rocket science.

Some Things You Ought to Know

Much of the confusion over the Internet comes from two sources. One is terminology. Just as the career you're preparing for has its own special vocabulary, so does the Internet. You'd be hard pressed to join in the shoptalk of archeologists, librarians, or carpenters if you didn't speak their language. Don't expect to plop yourself down in the middle of the Internet without some buzzwords under your belt, either.

The second source of confusion is that there are often many ways to accomplish the same ends on the Internet. This is a direct by-product of the freedom so highly cherished by Net citizens. When someone has an idea for doing something, he or she puts it out there and lets the Internet community decide its merits. As a result, it's difficult to put down in writing the *one exact* way to send email or find information on slugs or whatever.

In addition, there are differences in the workings of a PC or Mac and the various versions of the two major browsers, Netscape Communicator (or Navigator) and Internet Explorer. If you can't find a particular command or function mentioned in the book on your computer, chances are it's there, but in a different place or with a slightly different name. Check the manual or online help that came with your computer, or ask a more computer-savvy friend or professor.

And relax. Getting up to speed on the Internet takes a little time, but the effort will be well rewarded. Approach learning your way around the Internet with the same enthusiasm and curiosity you approach learning your way around a new college campus. This isn't a competition. Nobody's keeping score. And the only winner will be you.

In *Understanding Media,* Marshall McLuhan presaged the existence of the Internet when he described electronic media as an extension of our central nervous system. On the other hand, today's students introduced to the Internet for the first time describe it as "Way cool."

No matter which description you favor, you are immersed in a period in our culture that is transforming the way we live by transforming the nature of the information we live by. As recently as 1980, intelligence was marked by "knowing things." If you were born in that year, by the time you were old enough to cross the street by yourself, that definition had changed radically. Today, in a revolution that makes McLuhan's vision tangible, events, facts, rumors, and gossip are distributed instantly to all parts of the global body. The effects are equivalent to a shot of electronic adrenaline. No longer the domain of the privileged few, information is shared by all the inhabitants of McLuhan's global village. Meanwhile, the concept of information as intelligence feels as archaic as a television remote control with a wire on it (ask your parents about that).

With hardly more effort than it takes to rub your eyes open in the morning you can connect with the latest news, with gossip about your favorite music group or TV star, with the best places to eat on spring break, with the weather back home, or with the trials and tribulations of that soap opera character whose life conflicts with your history class.

You can not only carry on a real-time conversation with your best friend at a college half a continent away, but you can see and hear her, too. Or, you can play interactive games with a dozen or more worldwide, world-class, challengers; and that's just for fun.

When it comes to your education, the Internet has shifted the focus from amassing information to putting that information to use. Newspaper and magazine archives are now almost instantly available, as are the contents of many reference books. Distant and seemingly unapproachable experts are found answering questions in discussion groups or in electronic newsletters.

The Internet also addresses the major problem facing all of us in our split-second, efficiency-rated culture: Where do we find the time? The

Internet allows professors and students to keep in touch, to collaborate and learn, without placing unreasonable demands on individual schedules. Professors are posting everything from course syllabi to homework solutions on the Internet, and are increasingly answering questions online, all in an effort to ease the pressure for face-to-face meetings by supplementing them with cyberspace offices. The Internet enables students and professors to expand office hours into a twenty-four-hour-a-day, seven-day-a-week operation. Many classes have individual sites at which enrolled students can gather electronically to swap theories, ideas, resources, gripes, and triumphs.

By freeing us from some of the more mundane operations of information gathering, and by sharpening our information-gathering skills in other areas, the Internet encourages us to be more creative and imaginative. Instead of devoting most of our time to gathering information and precious little to analyzing and synthesizing it, the Internet tips the balance in favor of the skills that separate us from silicon chips. Other Internet citizens can gain the same advantage, however, and as much as the Internet ties us together, it simultaneously emphasizes our individual skills—our ability to connect information in new, meaningful, and exciting ways. Rarely have we had the opportunity to make connections and observations on such a wide range of topics, to create more individual belief systems, and to chart a path through learning that makes information personally useful and meaningful.

A Brief History of the Internet

The 20th century's greatest advance in personal communication and freedom of expression began as a tool for national defense. In the mid-1960s, the Department of Defense was searching for an information analogy to the new Interstate Highway System, a way to move computations and computing resources around the country in the event the Cold War caught fire. The immediate predicament, however, had to do with the Defense Department's budget, and the millions of dollars spent on computer research at universities and think tanks. Much of these millions was spent on acquiring, building, or modifying large computer systems to meet the demands of the emerging fields of computer graphics, artificial intelligence, and multiprocessing (where one computer was shared among dozens of different tasks).

While this research was distributed across the country, the unwieldy, often temperamental, computers were not. Though researchers at MIT had spare time on their computer, short of packing up their notes and traveling to Massachusetts, researchers at Berkeley had no way to use it. Instead, Berkeley computer scientists would wind up duplicating MIT hardware in California. Wary of being accused of re-inventing the wheel, the Advanced Research Projects Agency (ARPA), the funding arm of the Defense Department, invested in the ARPANET, a private network that would allow disparate computer systems to communicate with each other. Researchers could remain ensconced among their colleagues at their home campuses while using computing resources at government research sites thousands of miles away.

A small cadre of ARPANET citizens soon began writing computer programs to perform little tasks across the Internet. Most of these programs, while ostensibly meeting immediate research needs, were written for the challenge of writing them. These programmers, for example, created the first email systems. They also created games like Space Wars and Adventure. Driven in large part by the novelty and practicality of email, businesses and institutions accepting government research funds begged and borrowed their way onto the ARPANET, and the number of connections swelled.

As the innocence of the 1960s gave way the business sense of the 1980s, the government eased out of the networking business, turning the ARPANET (now Internet) over to its users. While we capitalize the word "Internet", it may surprise you to learn there is no "Internet, Inc.," no business in charge of this uniquely postmodern creation. Administration of this world-wide communication complex is still handled by the cooperating institutions and regional networks that comprise the Internet. The word "Internet" denotes a specific interconnected network of networks, and not a corporate entity.

Using the World Wide Web for Research

Just as no one owns the worldwide communication complex that is the Internet, there is no formal organization among the collection of hundreds of thousands of computers that make up the part of the Net called the World Wide Web.

If you've never seriously used the Web, you are about to take your first steps on what can only be described as an incredible journey. Initially, though, you might find it convenient to think of the Web as a giant television network with millions of channels. It's safe to say that, among all these channels, there's something for you to watch. Only, how to find it? You could click through the channels one by one, of course, but by the time you found something of interest it would (1) be over or (2) leave you wondering if there wasn't something better on that you're missing.

A more efficient way to search for what you want would be to consult some sort of TV listing. While you could skim through pages more rapidly than channels, the task would still be daunting. A more creative approach would allow you to press a button on your remote control that would connect you to a channel of interest; what's more, that channel would contain the names (or numbers) of other channels with similar programs. Those channels in turn would contain information about other channels. Now you could zip through this million-channel universe, touching down only at programs of potential interest. This seems far more effective than the hunt-and-peck method of the traditional couch potato.

If you have a feel for how this might work for television, you have a feel for what it's like to journey around (or surf) the Web. Instead of channels on the Web, we have *Web sites.* Each site contains one or more *pages.* Each page may contain, among other things, links to other pages, either in the same site or in other sites, anywhere in the world. These other pages may elaborate on the information you're looking at or may direct you to related but not identical information, or even provide contrasting or contradictory points of view; and, of course, these pages could have links of their own.

Web sites are maintained by businesses, institutions, affinity groups, professional organizations, government departments, and ordinary people anxious to express opinions, share information, sell products, or provide services. Because these Web sites are stored electronically, updating them is more convenient and practical than updating printed media. That makes Web sites far more dynamic than other types of research material you may be used to, and it means a visit to a Web site can open up new opportunities that weren't available as recently as a few hours ago.

Hypertext and Links

The invention that unveils these revolutionary possibilities is called *hypertext.* Hypertext is a technology for combining text, graphics, sounds, video, and links on a single World Wide Web page. Click on a link and you're transported, like Alice falling down the rabbit hole, to a new page, a new address, a new environment for research and communication.

Links come in three flavors: text, picture, and hot spot. A text link may be a letter, a word, a phrase, a sentence, or any contiguous combination of text characters. You can identify text links at a glance because

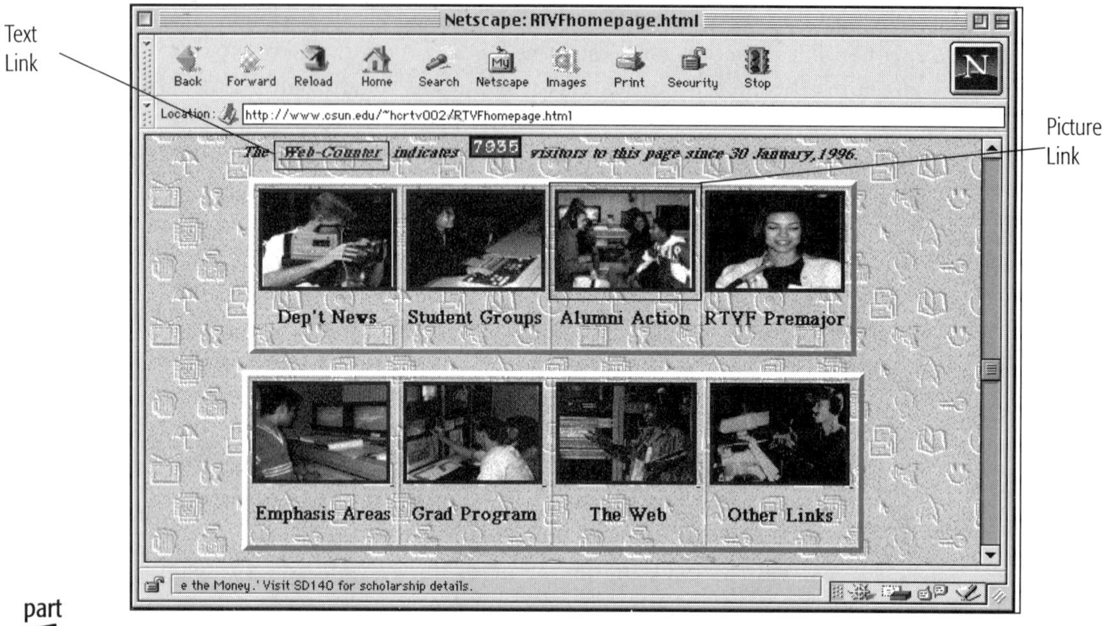

Text links are underlined and set of in color. Picture links are set off by a colored border. Hot spots carry no visual identification.

the characters are underlined, and are often displayed in a unique color, setting the link apart from the rest of the text on the page. Picture links are pictures or other graphic elements. On the Web, a picture may not only be worth a thousand words, but it may also be the start of a journey into a whole new corner of cyberspace.

The third kind of link, the hot spot, is neither underlined nor bordered, a combination which would make it impossible to spot, were it not for a Web convention that offers you a helping hand finding all types of links. This helping hand is, well, a hand. Whenever the mouse cursor passes over a link, the cursor changes from an arrow to a hand. Wherever you see the hand icon, you can click and retrieve another Web page. Sweep the cursor over an area of interest, see the hand, follow the link, and you're surfing the Web.

In the Name of the Page

Zipping around the Web in this way may seem exciting, even serendipitous, but it's also fraught with perils. How, for instance, do you revisit a page of particular interest? Or share a page with a classmate? Or cite a page as a reference for a professor? Web page designers assign names, or titles, to their pages; unfortunately, there's nothing to prevent two designers from assigning the same title to different pages.

An instrument that uniquely identifies Web pages does exist. It's called a Universal Resource Locator (URL), the cyber-signposts of the World Wide Web. URLs contain all the information necessary to locate:

- the page containing the information you're looking for;
- the computer that hosts (stores) that page of information;
- the form the information is stored in.

A typical URL looks like this:

```
http://www.abacon.com/index.html
```

You enter it into the **Location** or **Address** field at the top of your browser window. Hit the **Return** (or **Enter**) key and your browser will deliver to your screen the exact page specified. When you click on a link, you're actually using a shorthand alternative to typing the URL yourself because the browser does it for you. In fact, if you watch the "Location" or "Address" field when you click on a link, you'll see its contents change to the URL you're traveling to.

The URL Exposed

How does your browser—or the whole World Wide Web structure, for that matter—know where you're going? As arcane as the URL appears, there is a logical explanation to its apparent madness. (This is true not only of URLs but also of your computer experience in general. Because a computer's "intelligence" only extends to following simple instructions exactly, most of the commands, instructions, and procedures you'll encounter have simple underlying patterns. Once you familiarize yourself with these patterns, you'll find you're able to make major leaps in your understanding of new Internet features.)

To unscramble the mysteries of World Wide Web addresses, we'll start at the end of the URL and work our way toward the front.

```
/index.html
```

This is the name of a single file or document. Eventually, the contents of this file/document will be transferred over the Internet to your computer.

However, because there are undoubtedly thousands of files on the Internet with this name, we need to clarify our intentions a bit more.

```
www.abacon.com
```

This is the name of a particular Internet *Web server,* a computer whose job it is to forward Web pages to you on request. By Internet convention, this name is unique. The combination of

```
www.abacon.com/index.html
```

identifies a unique file/document on a unique Web server on the World Wide Web. No other file has this combined address, so there's no question about which file/document to transfer to you.

The characters *http://* at the beginning of the URL identify the method by which the file/document will be transferred. The letters stand for HyperText Transfer Protocol.

Quick Check

Don't Be Lost In (Hyper)Space

Let's pause for a quick check of your Web navigation skills. Look at the sample web page on the next page. How many links does it contain?

Did you find all five? That's right, five:

- The word "links" in the second line below the seaside picture;
- The sentence "What about me?";
- The word "cyberspace" in the quick brown fox sentence;
- The red and white graphic in the lower left-hand corner of the page. The blue border around it matches the blue of the text links;
- The hot spot in the seaside picture. We know there's at least one link in the picture, because the cursor appears as a hand. (There may be more hot spots on the page, but we can't tell from this picture alone.)

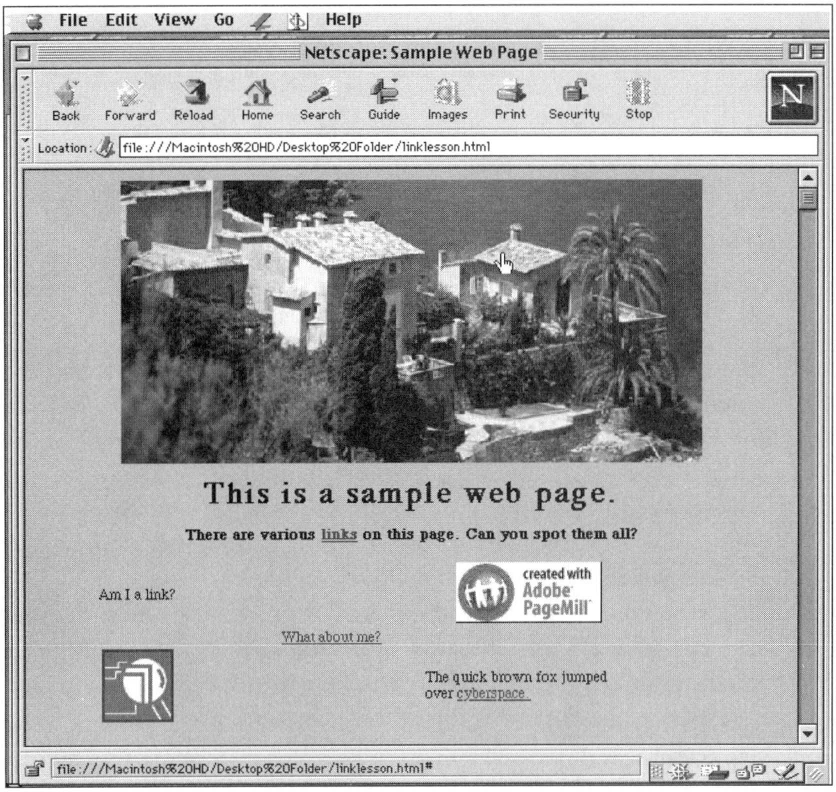

A sample web page to exercise your link identifying skills.

Getting There from Here

Now you know that a URL uniquely identifies a page and that links used as shorthand for URLs enable you to travel from page to page in the Web; but what if a link takes you someplace you don't want to go? Missing page messages take several forms, such as URL 404, Object not on this server, Missing Object, Page not Found, but they all lead to the same place—a dead end. The page specified by the link or URL no longer exists. There are many reasons for missing pages. You may have entered the URL incorrectly. Every character must be precise and no spaces are allowed. More than likely, though, especially if you arrived here via a link, the page you're after has been moved or removed. Remember, anybody can create a link to any page. In the spirit of the Internet, there are no forms to fill out, no procedures to follow. That's the good news. The bad news is that the owner of a page is under no

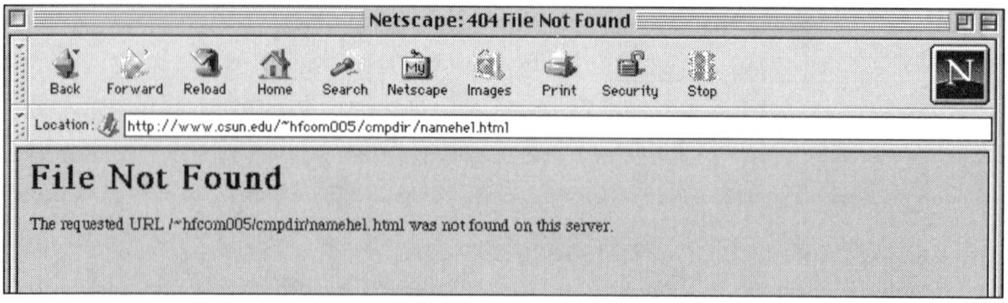

A missing page message, an all too common road hazard on the information superhighway.

obligation to inform the owners of links pointing to it that the page location has changed. In fact, there's no way for the page owner to even know about all the links to her page. Yes, the Internet's spirit of independence proves frustrating sometimes, but you'll find these small inconveniences are a cheap price to pay for the benefits you receive. Philosophy aside, though, we're still stuck on a page of no interest to us. The best strategy is to back up and try another approach.

part 1

Every time you click on the **Back** button, you return to the previous page you visited. That's because your browser keeps track of the pages you visit and the order in which you visit them. The **Back** icon, and its counterpart, the **Forward** icon, allow you to retrace the steps, forward and backward, of your cyberpath. Sometimes you may want to move two, three, or a dozen pages at once. Although you can click the **Back** or **Forward** icons multiple times, Web browsers offer an easier navigation shortcut. If you use Netscape, clicking on the **Go** menu in the menu bar displays a list of your most recently visited pages, in the order you've been there. Unlike the **Back** or **Forward** icons, you can select any page from the menu, and a single click takes you directly there. There's no need to laboriously move one page a time. If you use Internet Explorer, you can click on the **History** button in the Explorer bar to see a list of links you visited in previous days and weeks, or press the arrow at the end of the Address bar to see previously visited links.

Quick Check

As a quick review, here's what we know about navigating the Web so far:

- Enter a URL directly into the Location field;
- Click on a link;
- Use the **Back** or **Forward** icons;
- Select a page from the **Go** menu.

You Can Go Home (and to Other Pages) Again

How do we return to a page hours, days, or even months later? One way is to write down the URLs of every page we may want to revisit. There's got to be a better way, and there is: We call them bookmarks (on Netscape Communicator) or favorites (on Microsoft Internet Explorer).

Like their print book namesakes, Web bookmarks (and favorites) flag specific Web pages. Selecting an item from the **Bookmark/Favorites** menu, like selecting an item from the **Go** menu, is the equivalent of entering a URL into the **Location** field of your browser, except that items in the **Bookmark/Favorites** menu are ones you've added yourself and represent pages visited over many surfing experiences, not just the most recent one.

To select a page from your bookmark list, pull down the **Bookmark/Favorites** menu and click on the desired entry. To save a favorite page location, use the Add feature available in both browsers. In Netscape Communicator, clicking on the **Add Bookmark** command makes a bookmark entry for the current page. **Add to Favorites** performs the same function in Microsoft Internet Explorer. Clicking this feature adds the location of the current page to your **Bookmark/Favorites** menu.

A cautionary note is in order here. Your bookmark or favorites list physically exists only on your personal computer, which means that if you connect to the Internet on a different computer, your list won't be available. If you routinely connect to the Internet from a computer lab, for example, get ready to carry the URLs for your favorite Web sites in your notebook or your head.

Searching and Search Engines

Returning to our cable television analogy, you may recall that we conveniently glossed over the question of how we selected a starting channel in the first place. With a million TV channels, or several million Web pages, we can't depend solely on luck guiding us to something interesting.

On the Web, we solve the problem with specialized computer programs called *search engines* that crawl through the Web, page by page, cataloging its contents. As different software designers developed search strategies, entrepreneurs established Web sites where any user could find pages containing particular words and phrases. Today, Web sites such as Yahoo!, AltaVista, Excite, WebCrawler, and HotBot offer you a "front door" to the Internet that begins with a search for content of interest.

The URLs for some popular search sites are:

Excite	`www.excite.com`
Yahoo!	`www.yahoo.com`
AltaVista	`www.altavista.digital.com`
WebCrawler	`www.webcrawler.com`
MetaCrawler	`www.metacrawler.com`
Infoseek	`www.infoseek.com`
HotBot	`www.hotbot.com`

Internet Gold Is Where You Find It

Let's perform a simple search using HotBot to find information about the history of the Internet.

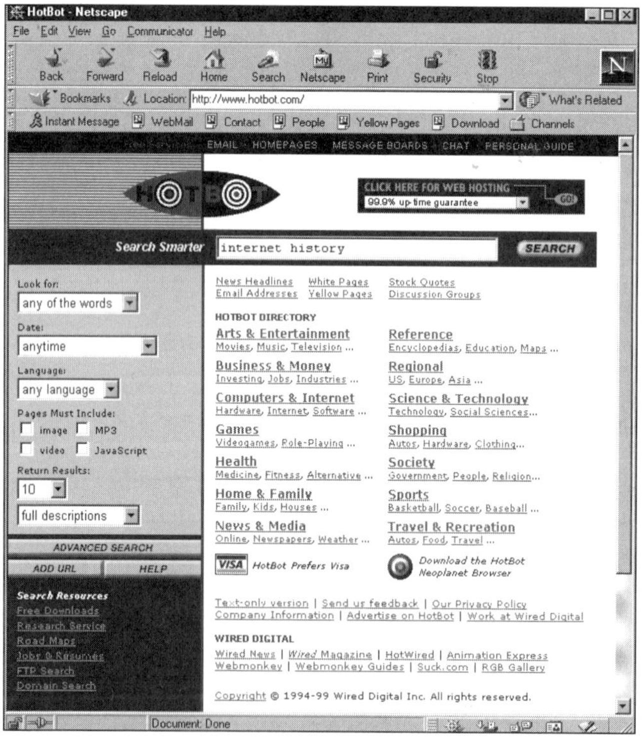

We'll start by searching for the words "internet" or "history." By looking for "any of the words," the search will return pages on which either "internet" or "history" or both appear.

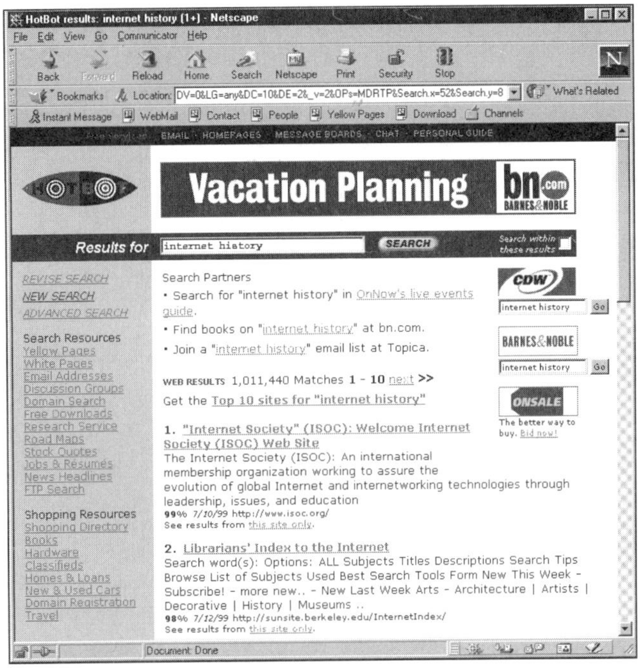

Our search returned 1,011,440 matches or *hits*. By viewing the percentage number in the last line of each summary, you will be able to see the "quality" of the match, which is usually related to the number of times the search word(s) appears on the page.

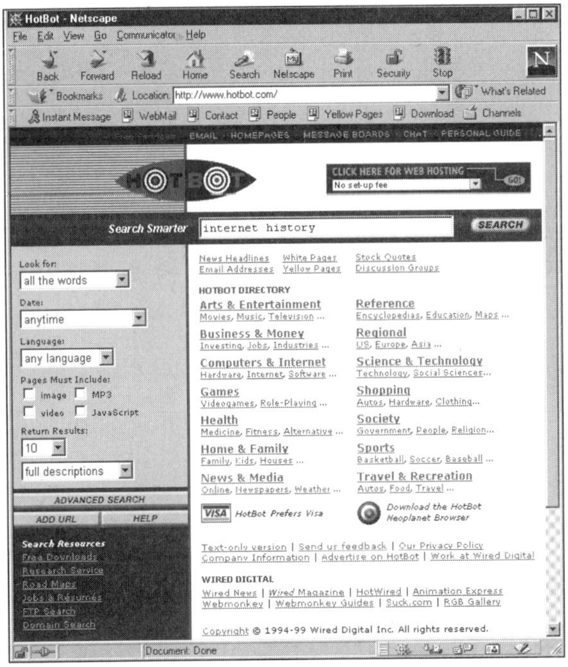

We can conduct the same search, but this time look for "all the words." The search will return hits when both "internet" and "history" appear on the same page, in any order, and not necessarily next to each other.

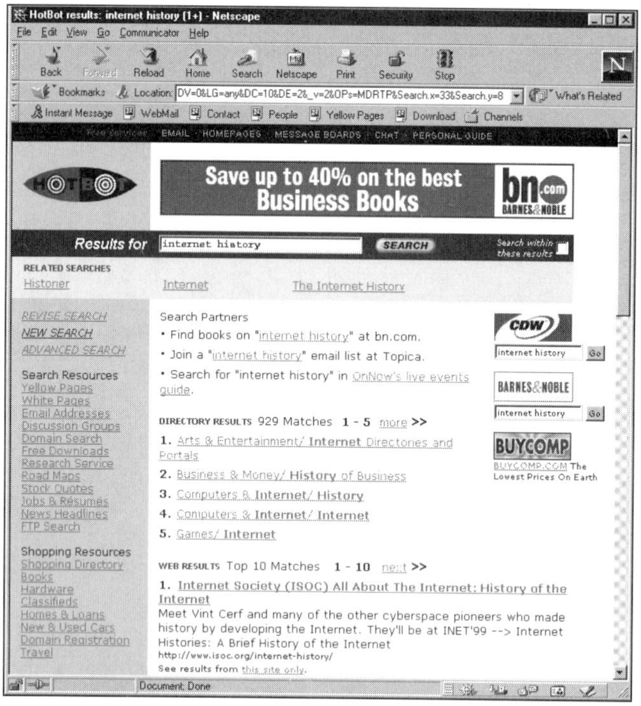

The search is narrowed down somewhat, but it is still not providing us with the information we need.

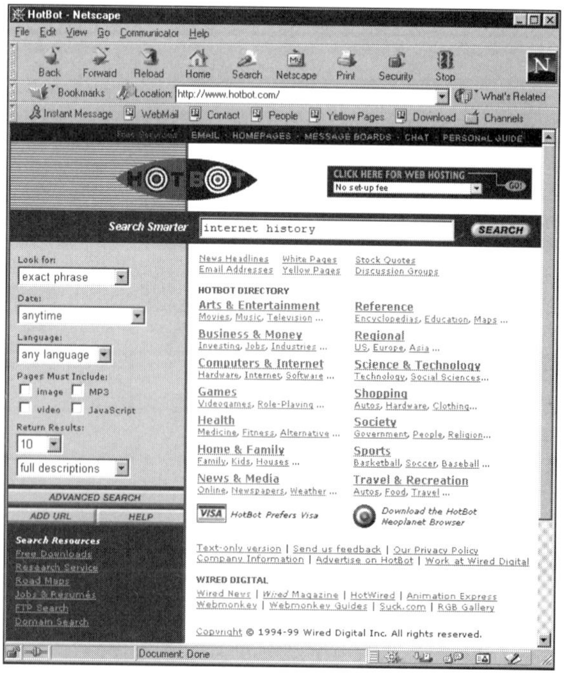

When we search for the exact phrase "internet history," which means those two words in exactly that order, with no intervening words, we're down to about 6,000 hits (still a substantial number).

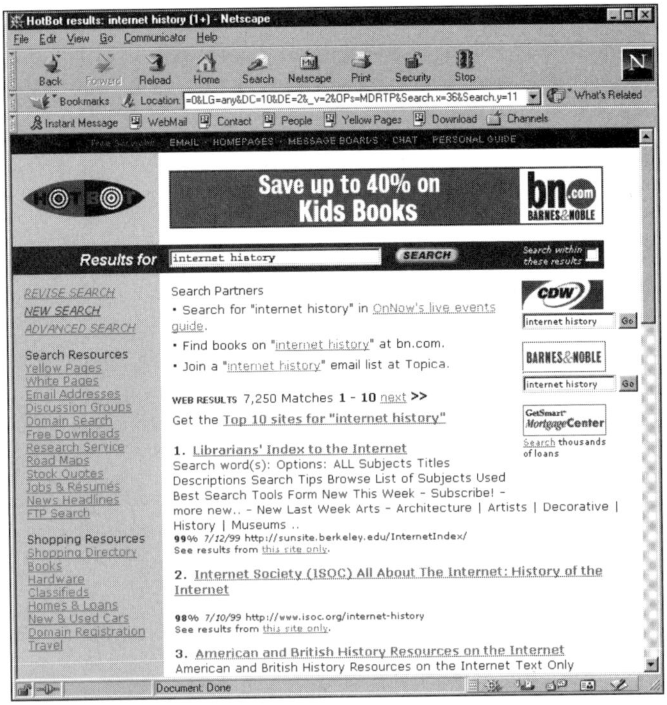

Now the first hits may be more specific. However, other hits in the list may have nothing to do with the history of the Internet. Hits happen. No search engine is 100 percent accurate 100 percent of the time. Spurious search results are the serendipity of the Internet. Look at them as an opportunity to explore something new.

Out of curiosity, let's try our history of the Internet search using a different search engine. When we search for the phrase "history of the internet" using WebCrawler, the quotation marks serve the same purpose as selecting "the exact phrase" option in Hotbot. The WebCrawler search only finds a few hundred hits. Some are the same as those found using HotBot, some are different. Different searching strategies and software algorithms make using more than one search engine a must for serious researchers.

The major search engines conveniently provide you with tips to help you get the most out of their searches. These include ways to use AND and OR to narrow down searches, and ways to use NOT to eliminate unwanted hits.

Each search engine also uses a slightly different approach to cataloging the Web, so at different sites your results might vary. Often, one search engine provides better results (more relevant hits) in your areas of interest; sometimes, the wise strategy is to provide the same input to several different engines. No one search engine does a perfect job all the time, so experience will dictate the one that's most valuable for you.

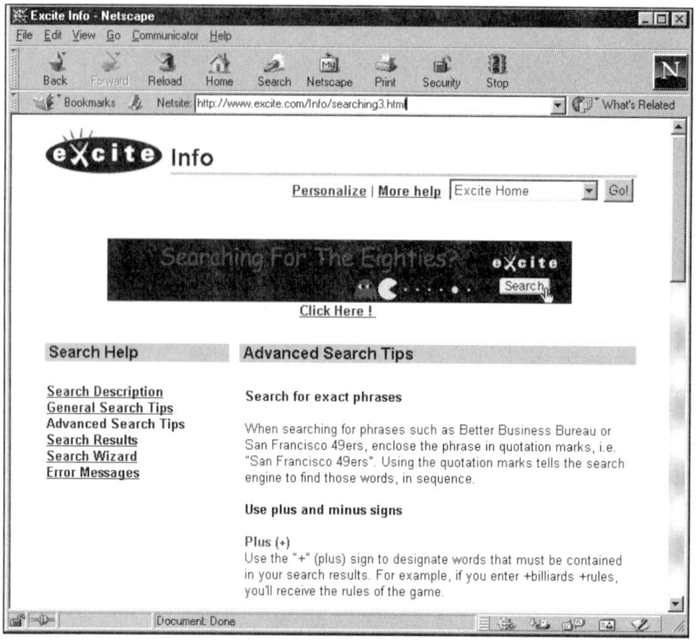

You'll find search tip pages like this at all the major search engine sites.

Quick Check

Let's review our searching strategies:

- Visit one of the search engine sites;
- Enter key words or phrases that best describe the search criteria;
- Narrow the search if necessary by using options such as "all the words" or "the exact phrase." On some search engines, you may use the word "and" or the symbol "|" to indicate words that all must appear on a page;
- Try using the same criteria with different search engines.

How Not to Come Down with a Virus

Downloading files from the Internet allows less responsible Net citizens to unleash onto your computer viruses, worms, and Trojan horses, all dangerous programs that fool you into thinking they're doing one thing while they're actually erasing your hard disk or performing some other undesirable task. Protection is your responsibility.

One way to reduce the risk of contracting a virus is to download software from reliable sites. Corporations such as Microsoft and Apple take care to make sure downloadable software is virus free. So do most institutions that provide software downloads as a public service (such as the Stanford University archives of Macintosh software). Be especially careful of programs you find on someone's home page. If you're not sure about safe download sources, ask around in a newsgroup (discussed shortly), talk to friends, or check with the information technology center on campus.

You can also buy and use a reliable virus program. Norton, Symantec, and Dr. Solomon all sell first-rate programs for the Mac and PC. You can update these programs right from the Internet so they'll detect the most current viruses. Most of the time, these programs can disinfect files/documents on your disk that contain viruses. Crude as it may sound, downloading programs from the Internet without using a virus check is like having unprotected sex with a stranger. While downloading software may not be life threatening, imagine the consequences if your entire hard disk, including all your course work and software, is totally obliterated. It won't leave you feeling very good.

If you'd like some entertaining practice sharpening your Web searching skills, point your browser to <www.internettreasurehunt.com>, follow the directions, and you're on your way to becoming an Internet researcher extraordinaire.

The (E)mail Goes Through

Email was one of the first applications created for the Internet by its designers, who sought a method of communicating with each other directly from their keyboards. Your electronic Internet mailbox is to email what a post office box is to "snail mail" (the name Net citizens apply to ordinary, hand-delivered mail). This mailbox resides on the computer of your Internet Service Provider (ISP). That's the organization providing you with your Internet account. Most of the time your ISP will be your school; but, you may contract with one of the commercial providers, such as America Online, Mindspring, Microsoft Network, Earthlink, or AT&T. The Internet doesn't deliver a message to your door but instead leaves it in a conveniently accessible place (your mailbox) in the post office (the computer of your ISP), until you retrieve the mail using your combination (password).

If you currently have computer access to the Internet, your school or ISP assigned you a *user name* (also called a user id, account name, or account number). This user name may be your first name, your first initial and the first few characters of your last name, or some strange combination of numbers and letters only a computer could love. An email address is a combination of your user name and the unique address of the computer through which you access your email, like this:

```
username@computername.edu
```

The three letters after the dot, in this case "edu," identify the top level "domain." There are six common domain categories in use: edu (educational), com (commercial), org (organization), net (network), mil (military), and gov (government). The symbol "@"—called the "at" sign in typewriter days—serves two purposes: For computers, it provides a neat, clean separation between your user name and the computer name; for people, it makes Internet addresses more pronounceable. Your address is read: user name "at" computer name "dot" e-d-u. Suppose your Internet user name is "a4736g" and your ISP is Allyn & Bacon, the publisher of this book. Your email address might look like

```
a4736g@abacon.com
```

and you would tell people your email address is "ay-four-seven-three-six-gee at ay bacon dot com."

We Don't Just Handle Your Email, We're Also a Client

You use email with the aid of special programs called *mail clients*. As with search engines, mail clients have the same set of core features, but your access to these features varies with the type of program. On both the PC and the Mac, Netscape Communicator and Microsoft Internet Explorer give you access to mail clients while you're plugged into the Web. That way you can pick up and send mail while you're surfing the Web.

The basic email service functions are creating and sending mail, reading mail, replying to mail, and forwarding mail. First we'll examine the process of sending and reading mail, and then we'll discuss how to set up your programs so that your messages arrive safely.

Let's look at a typical mail client screen, in this case from Netscape Communicator 4.6. You reach this screen by choosing **Messenger** from under the **Communicator** menu. To send a message from scratch, choose the **New Msg** button to create a blank message form, which has fields for the recipient's address and the subject, and a window for the text of the message.

Fill in the recipient's address in the "To" field, just above the arrow. Use your own address. We'll send email to ourselves and use the same

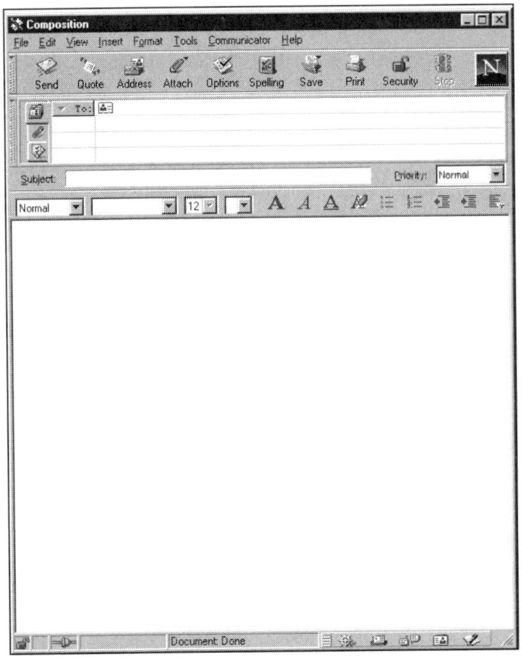

New message form, with fields for recipient's address and the subject, and a window for the text of the message.

message to practice sending email and reading it as well; then we'll know if your messages come out as expected.

Click in the "Subject" field and enter a word or phrase that generally describes the topic of the message. Since we're doing this for the first time, let's type "Maiden Email Voyage."

Now click anywhere in the text window and enter your message. Let's say "Hi. Thanks for guiding me through sending my first email." You'll find that the mail client works here like a word processing program, which means you can insert and delete words and characters and highlight text.

Now click the **Send** button on the Navigation toolbar. You've just created and sent your first email message. In most systems, it takes a few seconds to a few minutes for a message to yourself to reach your mailbox, so you might want to take a short break before continuing. When you're ready to proceed, close the **Composition** window and click the **Get Msg** button.

What Goes Around Comes Around

Now let's grab hold of the message you just sent to yourself. When retrieving mail, most mail clients display a window showing the messages in your mailbox telling you how many new messages have been added.

If you've never used your email before, chances are your message window is empty, or contains only one or two messages (usually official messages from the ISP) besides the one you sent to yourself. The message to yourself should be accompanied by an indicator of some sort—a colored mark, the letter N—indicating it's a new message. In Netscape Communicator, as in other mail clients, you also get to see the date of the message, who sent it, and the information you entered in the subject line. The Subject field lets you scan your messages and determine which ones you want to look at first.

The summary of received messages tells you everything you need to know about a message except what's in it. Click anywhere in the line to see the contents in the message window. Click on the message from yourself and you'll see the contents of the message displayed in a window. The information at the top—To, From, Subject, and so forth—is called the *header*. Depending on your system, you may also see some cryptic lines with terms such as X-Mailer, received by, and id number. Most of the time, there's nothing in this part of the header of interest, so just skip over it for now.

Moving Forward

The contents, or text, of your message can be cut and pasted just like any other text document. If you and a classmate are working on a project together, your partner can write part of a paper and email it to you, and you can copy the text from your email message and paste it into your word processing program.

What if there are three partners in this project? One partner sends you a draft of the paper for you to review. You like it and want to send it on to your other partner. The **Forward** feature lets you send the message intact, so you don't have to cut and paste it into a new message window. To forward a message, highlight it in the **Inbox** (top) and click the **Forward** icon. Enter the recipient's address in the "To" field of the message window. Note that the subject of the message is "Fwd:" followed by the subject of the original message. Use the text window to add your comments ahead of the original message.

A Chance to Reply

Email is not a one-way message system. Let's walk through a reply to a message from a correspondent named Elliot. Highlight the message in your **Inbox** again and this time click on the **Reply** icon. Depending on which program you're using, you'll see that each line in the message is preceded by either a vertical bar or a right angle bracket (>).

Note the "To" and "Subject" fields are filled in automatically with the address of the sender and the original subject preceded by "Re:". In Internet terminology, the message has been *quoted*. The vertical bar or > is used to indicate lines not written by you but by someone else (in this case, the message's original author). Why bother? Because this feature allows you to reply without retyping the parts of the message you're responding to. Because your typing isn't quoted, your answers stand out from the original message. Netscape Communicator 4.6 adds some blank lines above and below your comments, a good practice for you if your mail client doesn't do this automatically.

Welcome to the Internet, Miss Manners

While we're on the subject of email, here are some *netiquette* (net etiquette) tips.

- When you send email to someone, even someone who knows you well, all they have to look at are your words—there's no body language attached. That means there's no smile, no twinkle in the eye, no raised eyebrow; and especially, there's no tone of voice. What you write is open to interpretation and your recipient has nothing to guide him or her. You may understand the context of a remark, but will your reader? If you have any doubts about how your message will be interpreted, you might want to tack on an *emoticon* to your message. An emoticon is a face created out of keyboard characters. For example, there's the happy Smiley :-) (you have to look at it sideways . . . the parenthesis is its mouth), the frowning Smiley :-((Frownie?), the winking Smiley ;-), and so forth. Smileys are the body language of the Internet. Use them to put remarks in context. "Great," in response to a friend's suggestion means you like the idea. "Great :-(" changes the meaning to one of disappointment or sarcasm. (Want a complete list of emoticons? Try using "emoticon" as a key word for a Web search.)
- Keep email messages on target. One of the benefits of email is its speed. Reading through lengthy messages leaves the reader wondering when you'll get to the point.
- Email's speed carries with it a certain responsibility. Its ease of use and the way a messages seems to cry out for an answer both encourage quick responses, but quick doesn't necessarily mean thoughtful. Once you hit the **Send** icon, that message is gone. There's no recall button. Think before you write, lest you feel the wrath of the modern-day version of your parents' adage: Answer in haste, repent at leisure.

Keeping Things to Yourself

Here's another tip cum cautionary note, this one about Web security. Just as you take care to protect your wallet or purse while walking down a crowded street, it's only good practice to exercise caution with information you'd like to keep (relatively) private. Information you pass around the Internet is stored on, or passed along by, computers that are accessible to others. Although computer system administrators take great care to insure the security of this information, no scheme is completely infallible. Here are some security tips:

- Exercise care when sending sensitive information such as credit card numbers, passwords, even telephone numbers and addresses in plain email. Your email message may pass through four or five computers en route to its destination, and at any of these points, it can be intercepted and read by someone other than the recipient.
- Send personal information over the Web only if the page is secure. Web browsers automatically encrypt information on secure pages, and the information can only be unscrambled at the Web site that created the secure page. You can tell if a page is secure by checking the status bar at the bottom of your browser's window for an icon of a closed lock.
- Remember that any files you store on your ISP's computer are accessible to unscrupulous hackers.
- Protect your password. Many Web client programs, such as mail clients, have your password for you. That means anyone with physical access to your computer can read your email. With a few simple tools, someone can even steal your password. Never leave your password on a lab computer. (Make sure the **Remember Password** or **Save Password** box is unchecked in any application that asks for your password.)

The closed lock icon in the lower left-hand corner of your browser window indicates a "secure" Web page.

An Audience Far Wider Than You Imagine

Remember that the Web in particular and the Internet in general are communications mediums with a far-reaching audience, and placing information on the Internet is tantamount to publishing it. Certainly, the contents of any message or page you post become public information, but in a newsgroup (an electronic bulletin board), your email address also becomes public knowledge. On a Web page, posting a photo of your favorite music group can violate the photographer's copyright, just as if you published the image in a magazine. Use common sense about posting information you or someone else expects to remain private; and, remember, information on the Web can and will be read by people with different tastes and sensitivities. The Web tends to be self-censoring, so be prepared to handle feedback, both good and bad.

A Discussion of Lists

There's no reason you can't use email to create a discussion group. You pose a question, for example, by sending an email message to everyone in the group. Somebody answers and sends the answer to everyone else on the list, and so on.

At least, that's the theory.

In practice, this is what often happens. As people join and leave the group, you and the rest of your group are consumed with updating your lists, adding new names and deleting old ones. As new people join, their addresses may not make it onto the lists of all the members of the group, so different participants get different messages. The work of administering the lists becomes worse than any value anyone can get out of the group, and so it quickly dissolves.

Generally, you're better off letting the computer handle discussion group administration. A *list server* is a program for administering emailing lists. It automatically adds and deletes list members and handles the distribution of messages.

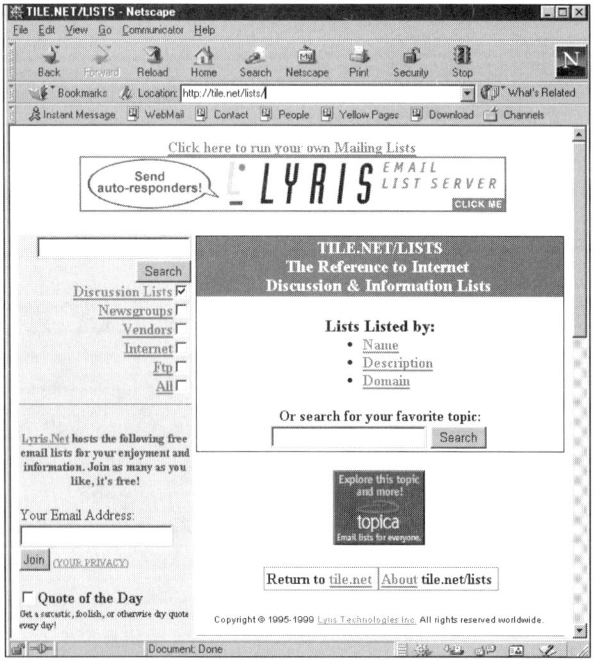

Tile.Net offfers shortcuts to working your way through the Internet's maze of discussion lists.

Thousands of mailing lists have already been formed by users with common interests. You may find mailing lists for celebrities, organizations, political interests, occupations, and hobbies. Your instructor may establish a mailing list for your course.

Groups come in several different flavors. Some are extremely active. You can receive as many as forty or more email messages a day. Other lists may send you a message a month. One-way lists, such as printed newsletters, do not distribute your reply to any other subscriber. Some lists distribute replies to everyone. These lists include mediated lists, in which an "editor" reviews each reply for suitability (relevance, tone, use of language) before distributing the message, and unmediated lists, in which each subscriber's response is automatically distributed to all the other subscribers with no restrictions except those dictated by decency and common sense, though these qualities may not always be obvious from reading the messages.

Get on a List Online

You join in the discussion by subscribing to a list, which is as straightforward as sending email. You need to know only two items: the name of the list and the address of the list server program handling subscriptions. To join a list, send a **Subscribe** message to the list server address. The message must contain the letters "Sub," the name of the list, and your name (your real name, not your user name), all on one line. *And that's all.* This message will be read by a computer program that looks for these items only. At the very best, other comments in the message will be ignored. At the very worst, your entire message will be ignored, and so will you.

Within a few hours to a day after subscribing, the list server will automatically send you a confirmation email message, including instructions for sending messages, finding out information about the list and its members, and canceling your subscription. Save this message for future reference. That way, if you do decide to leave the list, you won't have to circulate a message to the members asking how to unsubscribe, and you won't have to wade through fifty replies all relaying the same information you received when you joined.

Soon after your confirmation message appears in your mailbox, and depending on the activity level of the list, you'll begin receiving email messages. New list subscribers customarily wait a while before joining the discussion. After all, you're electronically strolling into a room full of strangers; it's only fair to see what topics are being discussed before wading in with your own opinions. Otherwise, you're like the bore at the party who elbows his way into a conversation with "But enough about you, let's talk about me." You'll also want to avoid the faux pas of posting a long missive on a topic that subscribers spent the preceding three weeks thrashing out. Observe the list for a while, understand its tone and feel, what topics are of interest to others and what areas are taboo. Also, look for personalities. Who's the most vociferous? Who writes very little but responds thoughtfully? Who's the most flexible? The most rigid? Most of all, keep in mind that there are far more observers than participants. What you write may be read by 10 or 100 times more people than those whose names show up in the daily messages.

When you reply to a message, you reply to the list server address, not to the address of the sender (unless you intend for your communication to remain private). The list server program takes care of distributing your message listwide. Use the address in the "Reply To" field of the message. Most mail clients automatically use this address when you select the **Reply** command. Some may ask if you want to use the reply address (say yes). Some lists will send a copy of your reply to you so you know your message is online. Others don't send the author a copy, relying on your faith in the infallibility of computers.

In the words of those famous late night television commercials, you can cancel your subscription at any time. Simply send a message to the address you used to subscribe (which you'll find on that confirmation message you saved for reference), with "Unsub," followed on the same line by the name of the list. For example, to leave a list named "WRITER-L," you would send:

```
Unsub WRITER-L
```

Even if you receive messages for a short while afterwards, have faith—they will disappear.

Waste Not, Want Not

List servers create an excellent forum for people with common interests to share their views; however, from the Internet standpoint, these lists are terribly wasteful. First of all, if there are one thousand subscribers to a list, every message must be copied one thousand times and distributed over the Internet. If there are forty replies a day, this one list creates forty thousand email messages. Ten such lists mean almost a half million messages, most of which are identical, flying around the Net.

Another wasteful aspect of list servers is the way in which messages are answered. The messages in your mailbox on any given day represent a combination of new topics and responses to previous messages. But where are these previous messages? If you saved them, they're in your email mailbox taking up disk space. If you haven't saved them, you have nothing to compare the response to. What if a particular message touches off a chain of responses, with subscribers referring not only to the source message but to responses as well? It sounds like the only safe strategy is to save every message from the list, a suggestion as absurd as it is impractical.

What we really need is something closer to a bulletin board than a mailing list. On a bulletin board, messages are posted once. Similar notices wind up clustered together. Everyone comes to the same place to read or post messages.

And Now the News(group)

The Internet equivalent of the bulletin board is the Usenet or newsgroup area. Usenet messages are copied only once for each ISP supporting the newsgroup. If there are one thousand students on your campus reading the same newsgroup message, there need only be one copy of the message stored on your school's computer.

Categorizing a World of Information

Newsgroups are categorized by topics, with topics broken down into subtopics and sub-subtopics. For example, you'll find newsgroups devoted to computers, hobbies, science, social issues, and "alternatives." Newsgroups in this last category cover a wide range of topics that may not appeal to the mainstream. Also in this category are beginning newsgroups.

Usenet names are amalgams of their topics and subtopics, separated by dots. If you were interested in a newsgroup dealing with, say, music, you might start with rec.music and move down to rec.music.radiohead, or rec.music.techno, and so forth. The naming scheme allows you to zero in on a topic of interest.

Getting into the News(group) Business

Most of the work of reading, responding to, and posting messages is handled by a news reader client program, accessible through both Netscape Communicator and Microsoft Internet Explorer. You can not only surf the Web and handle your mail via your browser, but you can also drop into your favorite newsgroups virtually all in one operation.

Let's drop into a newsgroup. To reach groups via Netscape Communicator 4.6, go to the Communicator menu bar and select **Newsgroups.** Then, from the File menu, select **Subscribe.** A dialogue box will open that displays a list of available groups.

To subscribe to a newsgroup—that is, to tell your news reader you want to be kept up-to-date on the messages posted to a particular group—highlight the group of interest and click on **Subscribe.** Alternately, you can click in the Subscribe column to the right of the group name. The check mark in the Subscribe column means you're "in."Now, click **OK.**

The message center in Netscape Communicator displays a list of newsgroups on your subscription list. Double click on the one of current interest and your reader presents you with a list of messages posted on the group's bulletin board. Double click on a message to open its contents in a window.

Often, messages contain "Re:" in their subject lines, indicating a response to a previous message (the letters stand for "Regarding"). Many news readers maintain a *thread* for you. Threads are chains of messages and all responses to that message. These readers give you the option to read messages chronologically or to read a message followed by its responses.

When you subscribe to a newsgroup, your news reader will also keep track of the messages you've read so that it can present you with the newest (unread) ones. While older messages are still available to you, this feature guarantees that you stay up-to-date without any record keeping on your part. Subscribing to a newsgroup is free, and the subscription information resides on your computer.

Newsgroups have no way of knowing who their subscribers are, and the same caveat that applies to bookmarks applies to newsgroups. Information about your subscriptions resides physically on the personal computer you're using. If you switch computers, as in a lab, your subscription information and history of read messages are beyond your reach.

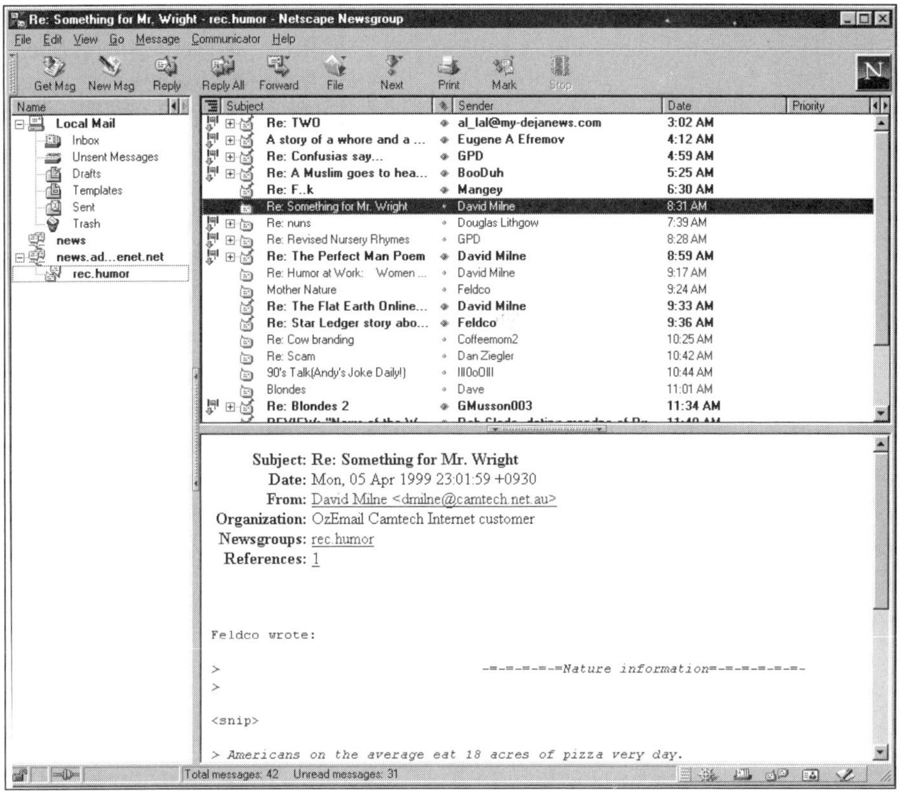

The top part of this figure shows a listing of posted messages. While not visible from this black and white reproduction, a red indicator in the Subject column marks unread messages. Double-clicking on a message opens its contents into a window shown in the bottom part of this figure. You can reply to this message via the Reply icon, or get the next message using the Next icon.

Welcome to the Internet, Miss Manners—Again

As with list servers, hang out for a while, or *lurk*, to familiarize yourself with the style, tone, and content of newsgroup messages. As you probably surmised from the names of the groups, their topics of discussion are quite narrow. One of the no-nos of newsgroups is posting messages on subjects outside the focus of the group. Posting off-topic messages, especially lengthy ones, is an excellent way to attract a flaming.

A *flame* is a brutally debasing message from one user to another. Flames are designed to hurt and offend, and often the target of the flame feels compelled to respond in kind to protect his or her self-esteem. This leads to a *flame war,* as other users take sides and wade in with flames of their own. If you find yourself the target of a flame, your best strategy is to ignore it. As with a campfire, if no one tends to the flames, they soon die out.

As mentioned earlier, posting messages to newsgroups is a modern form of publishing, and a publisher assumes certain responsibilities. You have a duty to keep your messages short and to the point. Many newsgroup visitors connect to the Internet via modems. Downloading a day's worth of long postings, especially uninteresting ones, is annoying and frustrating. Similarly, don't post the same message to multiple, related newsgroups. This is called *cross posting,* and it's a peeve of Net citizens who check into these groups. If you've ever flipped the television from channel to channel during a commercial break only to encounter the same commercial (an advertising practice called *roadblocking*), you can imagine how annoying it is to drop in on several newsgroups only to find the same messages posted to each one.

With the huge potential audience newsgroups offer, you might think you've found an excellent medium for advertising goods or services. After all, posting a few messages appears analogous to running classified ads in newspapers, only here the cost is free. There's a name for these kinds of messages—*spam.* Spam is the junk mail of the Internet, and the practice of spamming is a surefire way to attract flames. The best advice for handling spam? Don't answer it. Not only does an answer encourage the spammer, but he or she will also undoubtedly put your email address on a list and sell it to other spammers, who will flood your online mailbox with their junk.

Above all, be considerate of others. Treat them the way you'd like to be treated. Do you enjoy having your grammar or word choices corrected in front of the whole world? Do you feel comfortable when someone calls you stupid in public? Do you appreciate having your religion, ethnicity, heritage, or gender belittled in front of an audience? Respect the rights and feelings of others, if not out of simple decency then out of the sanctions your ISP may impose. Although you have every right to express an unpopular opinion or to take issue with the postings of others, most ISPs have regulations about the kinds of messages one can send via their facilities. Obscenities, threats, and spam may, at a minimum, result in your losing your Internet access privileges.

Give Your Web Browser Some Personality—Yours

Before accessing email and newsgroup functions, you need to set up or personalize your browser. If you always work on the same personal computer, this is a one-time operation that takes only a few minutes. In it, you tell your browser where to find essential computer servers, along with personal information the Internet needs to move messages for you.

- *Step 1:* Open the **Preferences** menu in Netscape or the **Internet Options** in Internet Explorer. In Netscape Communicator the Preferences menu is located under the **Edit** menu; in Microsoft Internet Explorer the Internet Options can be found under the **View** menu.
- *Step 2:* Tell the browser who you are and where to find your mail servers. Your Reply To address is typically the same as your email address, though if you have an email alias you can use it here. Microsoft Internet Explorer has slots for your mail servers in the same window. Your ISP will provide the server names and addresses. Be sure to use your user name (and not your alias) in the "Account Name" field. SMTP handles your outgoing messages, while the POP3 server routes incoming mail. Often, but not always, these server names are the same. Netscape Communicator has a separate window for server names.
- *Step 3:* Tell the browser where to find your news server. Your ISP will furnish the name of the server. Note that in Microsoft Internet Explorer, you specify a helper application to read the news. Now that most computers come with browsers already loaded onto the hard disk, you'll find that these helper applications are already set up for you.
- *Step 4:* Set your home page. For convenience, you may want your browser to start by fetching a particular page, such as your favorite search site. Or you might want to begin at your school library's home page. Enter the URL for this starting page in the home page address field. Both Netscape and Microsoft offer the option of no home page when you start up. In that case, you get a blank browser window.

Operating systems such as Mac OS 8 and Microsoft Windows 95 and 98 offer automated help in setting up your browsers for Web, mail, and newsgroup operation. You need to know the names of the servers mentioned above, along with your user name and other details, such as the address of the domain name server (DNS) of your ISP. You should receive all this information when you open your Internet account. If not, ask for it.

Speech-Language Pathology and Audiology and the Internet

The Internet is a dynamic resource for information access. Use of its capabilities can be particularly valuable in the fields of Speech-Language Pathology and Audiology. Practice in the field of communication disorders includes a broad spectrum of theoretical, academic, and clinical knowledge. In addition, Speech-Language Pathology and Audiology are relatively young disciplines—only formally organized less than 60 years ago—so information development is rapid and still moving in new directions. The Internet can help you access some of the current discussion and latest developments in areas of interest to our professions.

However, the amount of information available through the Internet can also be intimidating and confusing. Use of these resources should go beyond compiling a list of URLs, printing out color copies of some of the best-looking Web pages, or sending email to relatives. The justification for your time and money spent in online Internet activities is the application of the resources you find there to learning and problem solving about services for persons with communication disorders. Our goals in using the Internet should be (1) to identify relevant resource sites, (2) to evaluate the integrity and value of information available at those sites, (3) to integrate the information obtained online with other information sources for learning and application to the practice of our professions.

This section contains some examples of how a student in Audiology or Speech-Language Pathology can use the Internet to help in academic and clinical work. Additional exercises in application of the Internet to the professions can be found in Part II of this text.

Applications of the Internet in Communication Disorders

Students in Communication Disorders may use Internet services which are often provided at little or no cost through their university. Many students have learned to access World Wide Web sites to obtain information for required reports on topics related to their coursework. Finding this type of information usually involves using a search engine such as Yahoo! or Excite. Students find that doing a keyword search is much the same as doing a search at their campus library. Examples of this type of search appear later in this text.

However, there are other uses of the Internet which can help the Communication Disorders student actually enroll in and complete coursework, gather information regarding the availability and relative merits of graduate training programs, get expert advice on working with patients in a clinical practicum experience, find a job, and negotiate salary and benefits. Some insight into these applications of the Internet follows.

Making the Right Choices

Speech-Language Pathology and Audiology are exciting and rewarding professions. They encompass a variety of job descriptions and employment venues. As a Communication Disorders professional, you can make any number of lateral moves within these fields as life and your interests dictate. However, you must first obtain a graduate degree in the field. Moreover, to ensure the widest opportunities possible, you may take the examination for the Certificate of Clinical Competence and complete a Clinical Fellowship Year under the aegis of the national organization, the American Speech-Language-Hearing Association. This entails hard work and time on your part. You can use the Internet to help you make a decision about whether such a career is right for you, to identify the graduate program which best suits your needs, to apply to a graduate program, to complete some of the requirements for your graduate education, and to find employment when you graduate.

Career Decisions

You will certainly have opportunities to observe the work of a speech-language pathologist (SLP) or audiologist (Aud) during your undergraduate education. You can also talk to your professors, supervisors, and clinicians working in the field regarding the advantages and disadvantages of this career choice. Your search for information about the professions might begin at the Web site of the national professional organization, the American Speech-Language-Hearing Association (ASHA). This site contains many pages of information designed for students, professionals, and consumers. Within ASHA'S student section, you'll find career information including descriptions of the professions of speech-language pathology, audiology and speech and hearing science, testimonials from persons who have chosen these careers, and a FAQ.

1. Within your Web browser, open the location <http://www.asha.org/students/careers/careers.htm>.
2. When the Career Information page appears, choose the link, "Information for Those Considering a Career." On that page, read the statements by speech-language pathologists and audiologists describ-

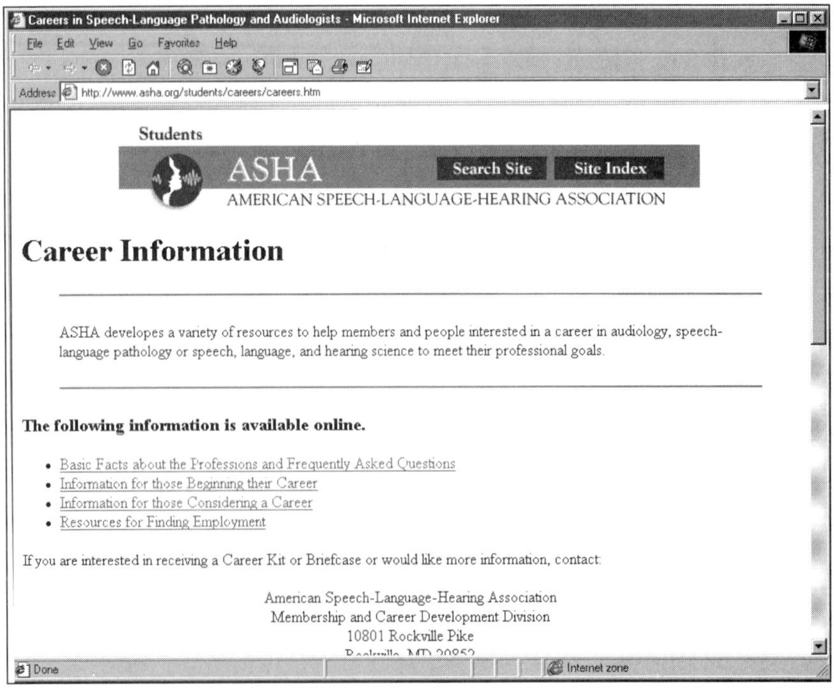

ing their reasons for selecting their career. Do any of their reasons appeal to you? Have they found the kind of experience that you feel is right for you?

3. Use your browser's "Back" option to return to the Career Information page, then select the link, "Basic Facts about the Professions and Frequently Asked Questions." You will find information on this page about the current job market for Communication Disorders personnel and a report on the average salary for persons working in the professions. Is it what you expected?

4. Find a second source of information on career opportunities using a search engine and keyword search items such as "career| audiology" (using the bar, but without the quotes). Compare the information found at this site to the information found at the ASHA career site.

5. Talk to your professors and to clinicians working in your community to compare their opinions about and experience in the profession to those presented in the ASHA Career Information page. Do they feel that the job market and salaries in the local community are comparable to the average reported at the national level? What were the career choices they made that directed them to their current position?

Graduate Training Programs in Communication Disorders

Your graduate education will entail a considerable investment of your time, money, and emotions. You will benefit from doing as much research as possible into the programs that are available to you. By beginning with the ASHA Web site, you can gather data on all the accredited Communication Disorders graduate training programs in the United States. You can contact these programs electronically to request detailed information regarding their admission standards, curricula, faculty, facilities, and application procedures. You may be able to communicate by email with individual faculty and students in these programs to determine if their program is the best fit for you.

1. Point your browser to <http://www.asha.org/students/caa_programs/caaprog.htm>. Here you will be able to select information on any of the Communication Disorders graduate programs in the United States by geographical region or state.

2. Select the region in which you want to attend graduate school by clicking on that region of the map on this page, or click on the state

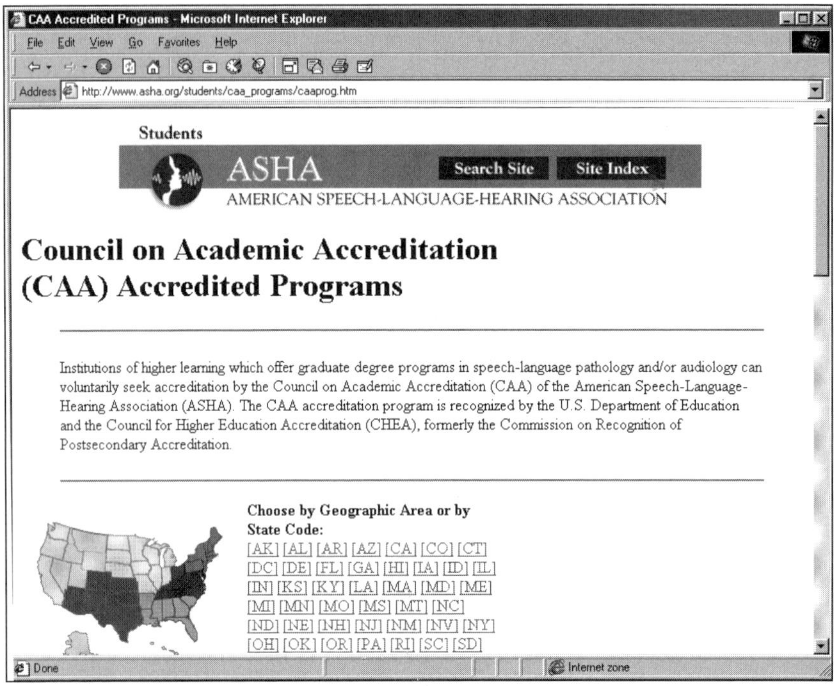

abbreviation if you have a particular state in mind. How many graduate programs are available there?

3. For some of these programs, a link to a specific information page is available describing admission standards, address to obtain an application, and program statistics such as admission rates, graduation rates, average GPA, and financial aid available. You can compare the programs by using the information on this page.

- For example, do some programs seem to consider qualifications in addition to test scores and GPA for admission to their program?
- What is the percentage of admissions relative to number of applicants?
- How many credit hours are required for earning a master's degree?
- How long does it take to complete the program of study?
- What are the research interests of the faculty?

3. Use your browser's "Back" button to return to the CAA Accredited Programs page, then click on the link "Why you should choose a CAA accredited program." Do you agree with the rationale presented on this page?

4. Following your review of the ASHA information on graduate programs, use a search engine such as AltaVista to find the URLs of the universities with the graduate programs that interest you.

- Can you electronically download or request an application packet from the university's graduate school?
- Is there information specific to the Communication Disorders program?
- Are there graphics of the campus and the facilities available to you?

5. Obtain an email address for the head of the Communication Disorders program or for one of the other faculty members. Let the person you contact know that you are interested in their program. Express your questions about and interests related to communication disorders to them. This electronic contact may be the next best thing to a campus visit for gaining recognition when application review time comes around!

Coursework on the Web

In addition to required coursework in your communication disorders training program, you may want to enroll in a course which offers specialized information not available to you on campus or one which can be taken through distance education while you are not enrolled in regular classes.

Sometimes these courses are available for academic credit toward graduation from your university. Information about courses which can be included in your program of study should be available from your academic advisor, from your university's distance education center or the computer and networking administrative unit on your campus. Some of these courses are available for enrollment at anytime during the year while others are offered only during a prescribed period. The courses may involve:

- live, interactive transmission between students at remote sites and an instructor on campus,
- one-way transmission which occurs only at a scheduled time at various reception sites within a geographical region,
- delivery of all instructional materials through Web site modules which can be accessed anytime within the course period.

Typically, the courses include assignments with requirements that can be fulfilled both electronically and with hard copy submissions. There will also be some form of evaluation of students' performance based on electronic examinations or live, proctored tests. The institution sponsoring the course should support the student through contact with the instructor or a teaching assistant by email and telephone. Assigned mentors or preceptors who can be contacted online and, perhaps, at a number of physical locations convenient to the enrollee, may also be available. Usually texts, study materials, and library support are also available to the student for these courses.

Other courses might serve to develop a personal and specialized interest of yours which will broaden your educational experience and help you perform at a higher level within your chosen field. For the Communication Disorders student, fields such as psychology, nursing, business, special education, or linguistics may offer an enriching educational experience. Such courses can be found through the on-campus resource personnel mentioned above or by doing an online search within the Education section of most Internet search engines using a keyword such as [online+coursesl "communication disorders"] (omit the brackets). An example of a Web site which presents information and links to many distance learning opportunities is <http://www.geteducated.com/dlsites.htm>.

The course "Internet Navigator" at <http://medstat.med.utah.edu/navigator/navigator.html> is an example of a course that might help you to hone your use of the Internet for use both as a student and in your professional life. You can enroll in this course for credit using the online registration process available for the State of Utah's universities.

1. Access this site and read through the introduction for the course, and the description of each of the course modules. Is the material in this course relevant for increasing your level of sophistication regarding Internet usage?
2. Which materials are accessible to you prior to registration for the course?
3. What are the advantages to you in completing the course registration?

The Best Job

Even before you finish your graduate degree, you will begin thinking about and preparing for your first job. Factors which you will want to consider will be type of work setting, geographic location, salary, benefits, availability of clinical fellowship supervision, and employer prefer-

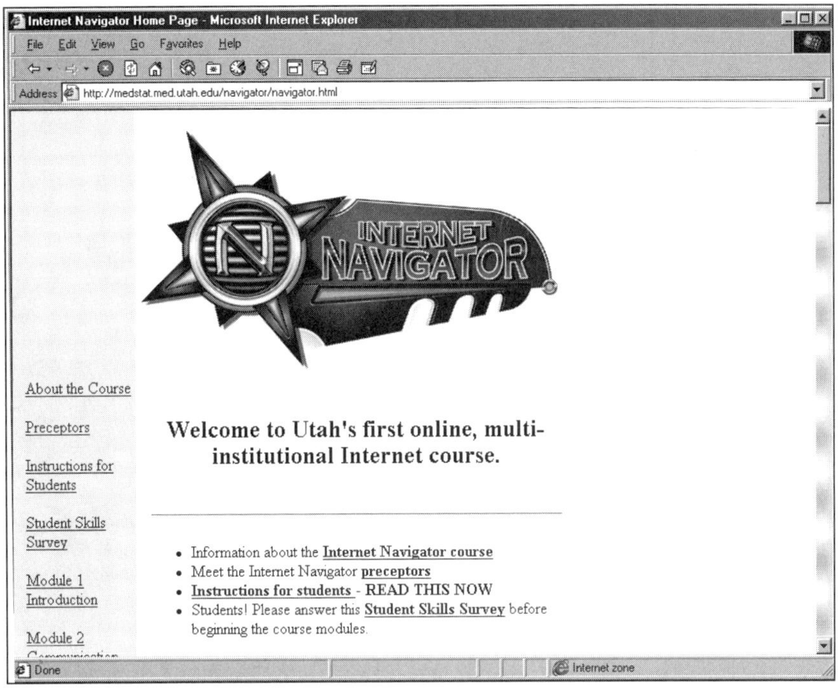

ences. There is information available on the Internet which can help you identify and prepare for obtaining the job which best suits your needs and preferences.

You might want to know what the current job market is like since this will determine how much bargaining power you have. One place to find current information is at the U.S. Department of Labor, Bureau of Labor Statistics.

1. Point your browser to <http://www.rehabjobs.com/joboutlook.html> where you will find the Occupation Outlook Handbook containing statistics related to employment for therapists. Choose the SLP and Aud page.
2. What is the job forecast for SLPs and Auds from the present to the year 2006?
3. How does the average salary for SLPs and Auds compare to those of other therapy-based professions presented at this Web site?

Of course, to get the job you want you will need to prepare and present yourself as well as possible. There is information online to help you do that.

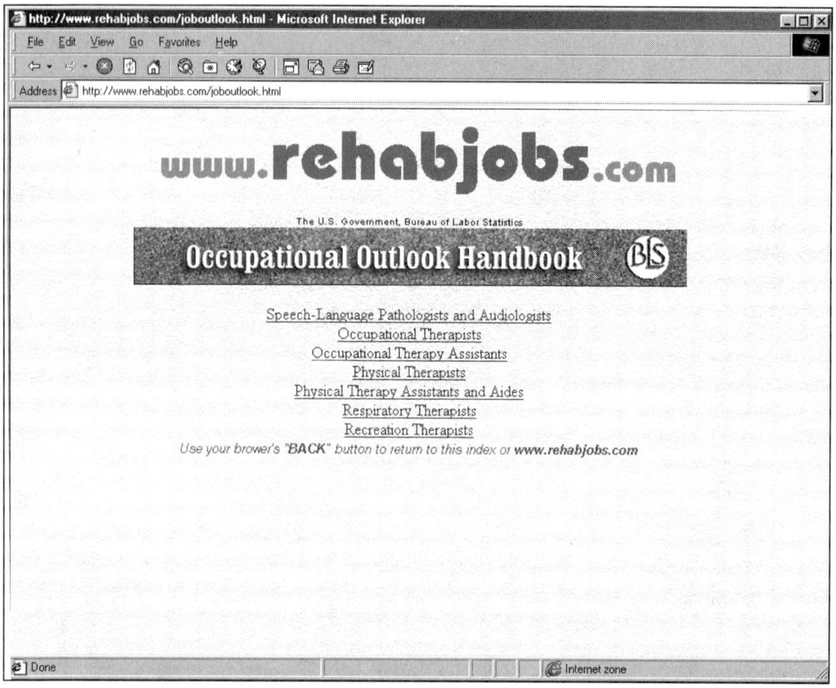
http://www.rehabjobs.com/joboutlook.html - Microsoft Internet Explorer
File Edit View Go Favorites Help
Address http://www.rehabjobs.com/joboutlook.html
www.rehabjobs.com
The U.S. Government, Bureau of Labor Statistics
Occupational Outlook Handbook
BLS
Speech-Language Pathologists and Audiologists
Occupational Therapists
Occupational Therapy Assistants
Physical Therapists
Physical Therapy Assistants and Aides
Respiratory Therapists
Recreation Therapists
Use your brower's "BACK" button to return to this index or www.rehabjobs.com
Done
Internet zone

part
1

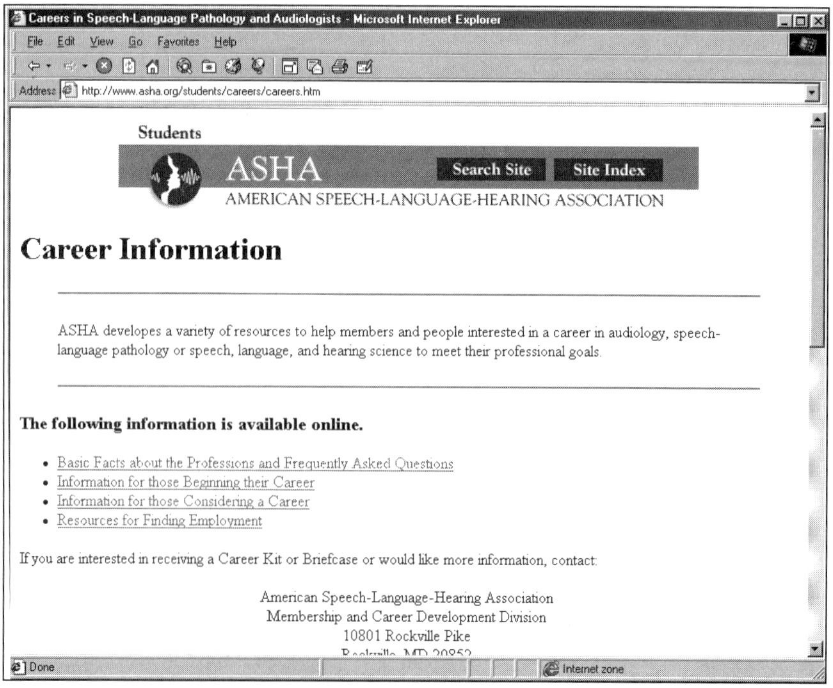
Careers in Speech-Language Pathology and Audiologists - Microsoft Internet Explorer
File Edit View Go Favorites Help
Address http://www.asha.org/students/careers/careers.htm
Students
ASHA
Search Site
Site Index
AMERICAN SPEECH-LANGUAGE-HEARING ASSOCIATION
Career Information
ASHA developes a variety of resources to help members and people interested in a career in audiology, speech-language pathology or speech, language, and hearing science to meet their professional goals.
The following information is available online.
Basic Facts about the Professions and Frequently Asked Questions
Information for those Beginning their Career
Information for those Considering a Career
Resources for Finding Employment
If you are interested in receiving a Career Kit or Briefcase or would like more information, contact:
American Speech-Language-Hearing Association
Membership and Career Development Division
10801 Rockville Pike
Done
Internet zone

1. Go to the ASHA Web site <http://www.asha.org/students/careers/careers.htm>.
2. On the page "Information for those beginning their career" you will find a description of some of the work settings in which SLPs and Audiologists typically are employed. Also found on this page is a delineation of factors to be considered when building a resume and interviewing for a job.
3. Which of the work settings descriptions sounds best to you, and why? Should this influence the kind of graduate program you will seek?
4. Can you formulate answers to the interview questions presented on this page?

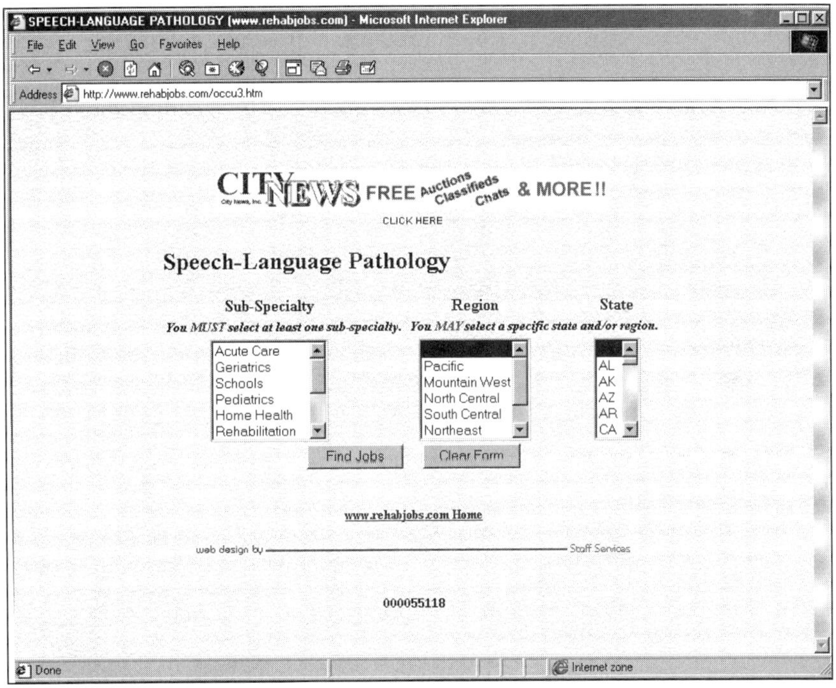

To find a specific job, you can search a database such as <http://www.rehabjobs.com/occu3.htm>. Here you will find a free listing of jobs in the health sector listed by region and state with online links to the employing agency.

1. Select each of the sub-specialty areas of practice, then click region or state in which you would like to work to see how many positions are advertised on this list.

2. Contact one of the agencies advertising at this site to gather more information about specific jobs available, salary range, sign-on bonus, etc.

You can also use the ASHA Web site to find a specific job through the classified advertisements in the *ASHA Leader.* The ads from the last two issues of the *Leader* are online. You can view all the ads contained in an issue, or search by state for a position. In addition, members of the National Student Speech-Language-Hearing Association can place their resume online in the ASHA Employment Referral Service database for 12 months at a cost of $11.00. If you would like to begin your search by networking with former graduates of your training program or with professionals already employed in a certain geographic area, you can use your NSSLHA membership number at this same site to do a search of the online *ASHA Membership Directory* for names, addresses, and contact numbers. ASHA members in your hometown might be willing to mentor you during your clinical fellowship year or would be able to tell you about the current job market in their area. There is also an excellent article by Judith Kuster on using Internet resources for job hunting in the Winter 1998 ASHA magazine.

If you are trying to decide in what geographic areas to job hunt, you might want some "life quality" information about the locations. Go to <http://www2.homefair.com/ calc/salcalc.html> where you will find information on cost of living differences between specific cities, moving costs, crime rate statistics, even comparative insurance rates.

1. If you moved from your hometown to Lexington, Kentucky, could you use the difference in cost of living to help you justify your negotiation for a higher salary?

2. Using the Salary Calculator, choose From (your home state) and then choose To (Kentucky).

3. Click on the "Show Cities" button.

4. From the list which appears, choose From (your hometown—or the closest city to it that appears on the list) and To (Lexington, Kentucky).

5. At the top of the Calculator, type in the starting salary you would like.

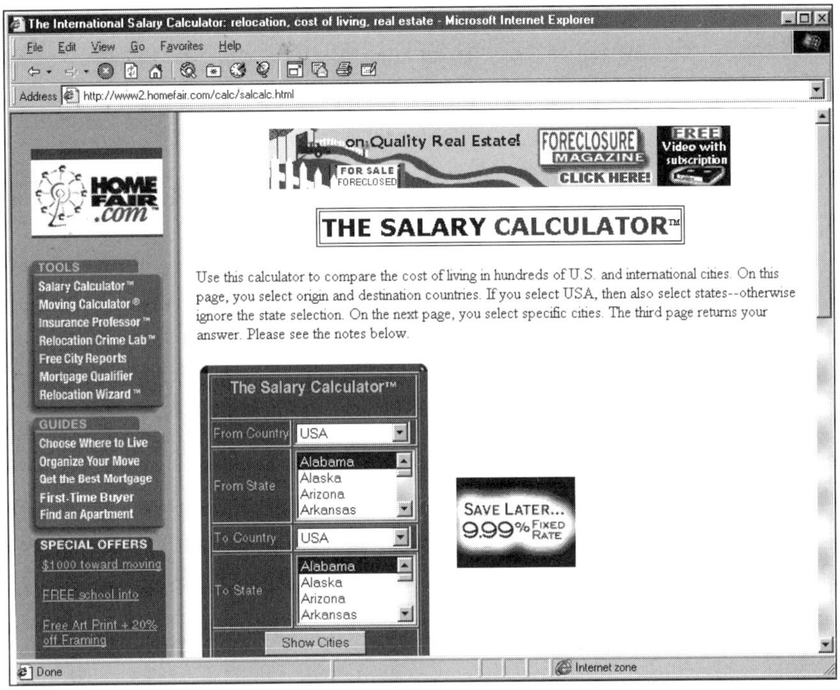

6. Click on the "Calculate" button, after which you will be shown the equivalent salary you would need to make in Lexington as compared to your hometown based on differences in cost-of-living factors.
7. Try the "Moving Calculator" or the "Relocation Crime Lab" information areas to get more information that might be used in job negotiations and decisions.

Finding Relevant Resources

Making the Grade

In your "Introduction to Speech Science" course, you've been required to produce an oral and written report about speech synthesis. Since much of the speech synthesis activity is related to text-to-speech conversion for computers, you decide that a computer-based report will be appropriate and more interesting than a paper-based report. Rather than presenting an online demonstration on your report day, you create a Web page combining text, graphics and links to relevant Web sites as the basis for your presentation. Since you don't have network connection capability in the classroom, you use a presentation program to display still shots, Quicktime movie clips and audio segments with some of the information available at your Web page.

part 1

1. Users of your Web page are first sent to the Museum of Speech Analysis and Synthesis <http://mambo.ucsc.edu/psl/smus/smus.html> where they can view photographs and drawings of some of the early mechanical attempts to produce synthesized speech, some were used over 100 years ago! By clicking on each graphic at the Museum, users can access textual descriptions of the machines, such as the Voder, and the work done with them during periods of historical development in speech synthesis. You also include links to Bell Laboratories <http://www.bell-labs.com/> and Haskins Laboratories <http://www.haskins.yale.edu/haskins/inside.html> where much of the keystone research in speech perception and production, a foundation for speech synthesis work, was completed. Both Web sites contain archived information and photographs of the pioneers in these areas, such as Cooper and Liberman, and bibliographies covering their research. There are some references in these bibliographies

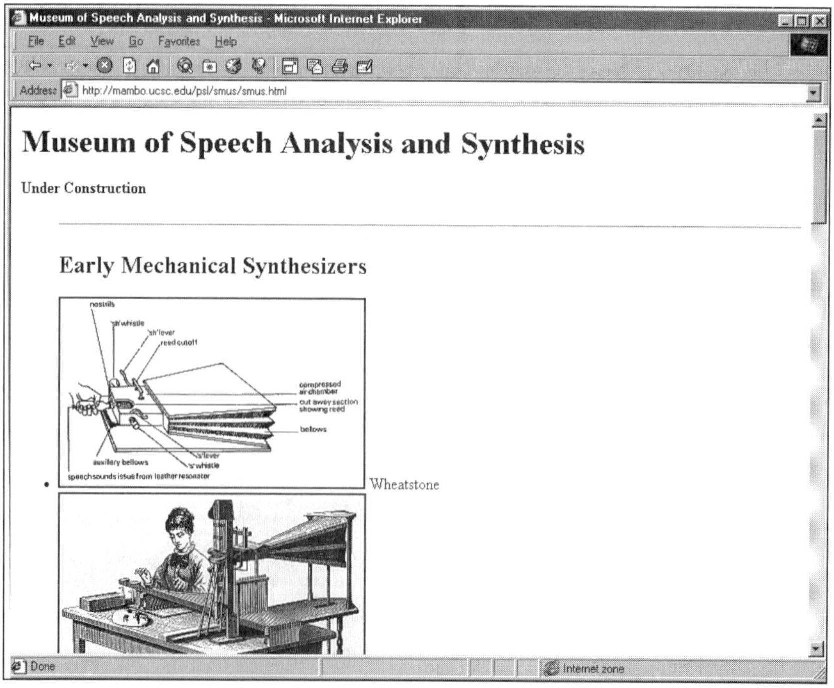

which you can use to build your own online bibliography about speech synthesis foundations as part of your Web page presentation.

2. Next, you send your Web page user to the Speech Synthesis FAQ Web site <http://svr-www.eng.cam.ac.uk/comp.speech/FAQ5.html> where they can access information on basic questions concerning speech synthesis. You have already gathered some of the reference sources listed here to build the online bibliography on speech synthesis which you provide on your Web page.

3. You've set up some listening links on your Web page so that users can hear examples synthesized speech samples available from current research projects. First, you go provide a link back to Bell Laboratories where online demonstration of text-to-speech synthesis is available. Next, at the Expressive Synthesized Speech site at Massachusetts Institute of Technology's Media Laboratory <http://cahn.www.media.mit.edu/people/cahn/emot-speech.html>, they can hear synthesized speech that has the added component of emotional overtone and read about how the research used the parameters of the voice, such as pitch, to create the perception of emotion. Both natural and synthesized sound files of pathological voices can be heard at the University of California, Los Angeles' Speech Processing and Auditory Perception Laboratory <http://www.icsl.ucla.edu/~spapl/>.

4. The final part of your Web-based presentation is a link to Speech On The Web <http://www.tue.nl/ipo/hearing/webspeak.htm> which is a jumpstation for speech synthesis. At this site, users can continue their exploration of synthesized speech and related areas such as phonetics and linguistics with a multitude of links to Web sites throughout the world.

5. Your professor has learned some things about speech synthesis that she didn't know existed. You get an "A+" on this assignment!

part 1

Current Theory and Practice

Speech-Language Pathology and Audiology students are often required to gather the most current information related to a specific topic or even a specific patient. In these specialty fields, information expands and changes rapidly requiring both students and practitioners to supplement their knowledge base by accessing dynamic information resources such as the Internet. For example, the student might be required to do a course presentation on research reports which have been published since the printing date of the text they use in a graduate course. One way to accomplish this is to do a general hunt using an Internet Search Engine. To hasten such a search, you could search using a web site that gives you access to a more specific subgroup—such as medicine—for several different search engines from the same page. You will save time by going to a single site for multiple searches rather than having to go to each search engine's individual site.

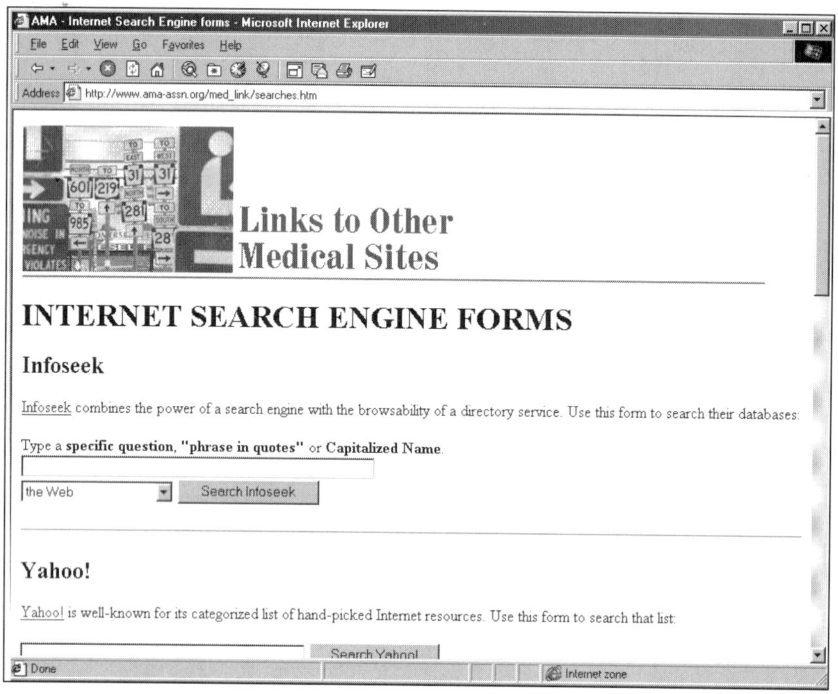

1. Find information related to laryngeal transplants.
2. Go to the American Medical Association's Web site and access the "Links to Other Medical Sites" page by pointing your browser to <http://www.ama-assn.org/med_link/searches.htm>.
3. Here you will find search links for a number of different search engines that can find information not only on the World Wide Web, but other electronic resources such as newsgroups as well.
4. Enter the key phrase "laryngeal transplant" (include the quotation marks) in at least three different search engines, then click their respective Search buttons.

5. Did each of the search engines you tried come up with the same citations?
6. Did each of the search engines you tried take a similar amount of time to complete the search?

Supplemental Learning

In some cases, students' experience with patients with low-incidence communication disorders or their access to certain medical procedures and instrumental techniques may be limited by the finances, library resources, or isolated location of their local college program. Students can supplement their educational experience by using the Internet to find, for example, online radiographic images of anatomical structures or to search a larger library database.

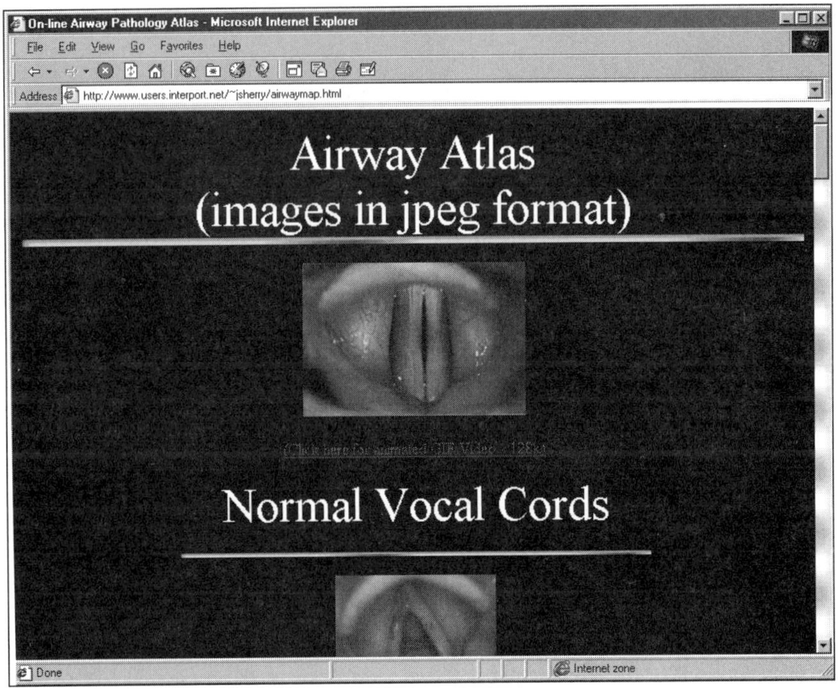

1. The resources available to as an undergraduate student in Communication Disorders may not include endoscopic views of the interior of the larynx which might help you to better understand the anatomy and physiology of voice production.

part 1

2. Point your browser to the Airway Atlas Web site <http://www.users.interport.net/ ~jsherry/airwaymap.html>, to see some telescopic views of the vocal folds and larynx obtained with laryngoscopy.
3. Click on the GIF animation sequence just below the normal larynx graphic to watch the vocal folds abduct and adduct.
4. Do these views of the normal larynx and laryngeal pathologies clarify your understanding of the effect such problems would have on the speaking voice?

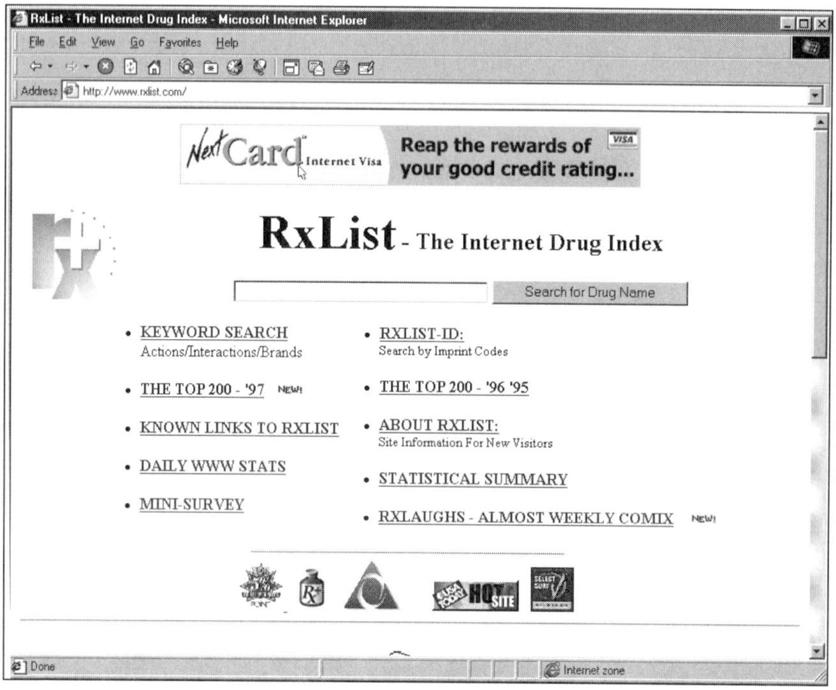

1. Your clinical practicum site may not have a current book on pharmacological agents and their effects. If you see a patient who reports regular use of an unfamiliar drug, you might want to know if the drug has any side effects which might affect your treatment plant.

2. Go to Rx Internet Drug Index <http://www.rxlist.com/> and do a search on the generic drug albuterol.

3. Select the link which appears for this drug.

4. Read the section on adverse reactions.

5. Do you see any indications that this might produce some secondary effects on voice production or hearing function?

Clinical Practice

The Internet can also be used to obtain specialized information and resources for students to use in their clinical practicum experiences. In clinical practicum, the patient assigned to a student for therapy might be diagnosed with a disease with which the student needs to become familiar for evaluation and treatment planning purposes. The student can go online to search for Web sites containing information on the disease or consult with experts in special interest listservs. (Always following strict clinical confidentiality guidelines, of course. Such online requests should be cleared by the student's clinical instructors.)

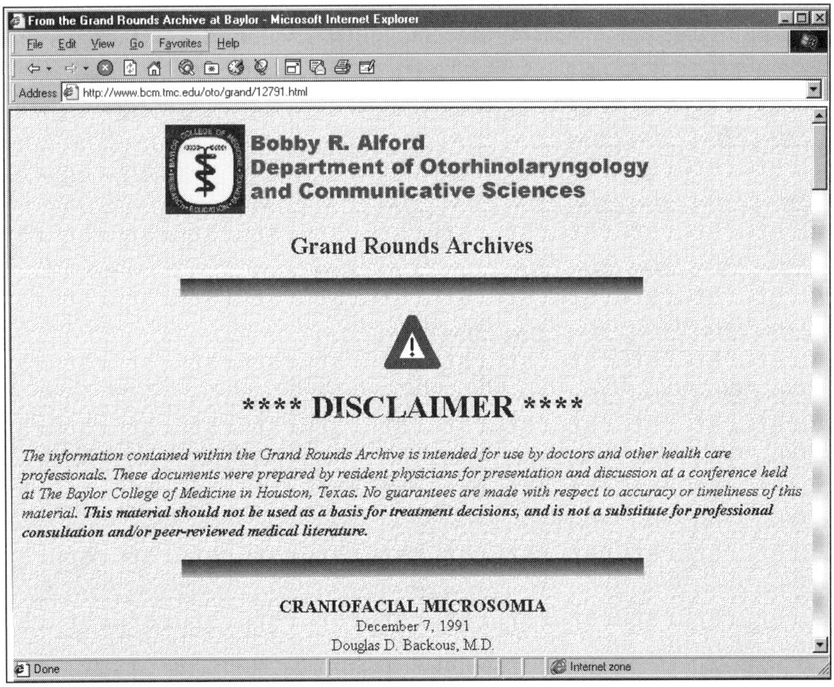

1. You have been assigned to do a speech evaluation on a 6-year old boy who is referred with a diagnosis of hemifacial microsomia. You know very little other than that it is a craniofacial malformation. You want more information so that you may prepare for the evaluation appropriately.
2. Go to Baylor College of Medicine's Grand Rounds Web site page on craniofacial microsomia by pointing your browser to <http://www.bcm.tmc.edu/oto/grand/12791.html>.
3. On this page, you will find a description of the disorder, a case study presentation and a list of references containing more detailed information.
4. What information do you find on this page that will help you plan the instruments and procedures you will use in your evaluation of this boy's speech?

In addition, therapy activity materials and consumer information can be downloaded from the Internet for the student to use in their clinical sessions with a patient. Both children and adult patients can be motivated to attend to a therapy task longer through the use of computer-delivered, multimedia stimulus/response materials. They can also access some of these materials independently in the classroom or at home for reinforcement, generalization and maintenance activities.

1. Point your browser to Berit's Best Sites for Children at <http://db.cochran.com/li_toc:theoPage.db>.
2. This is a jumpstation to many Internet locations some of which have online activity for children and some of which provide downloadable software for children.
3. As you work your way through the many categories such as "Just for Girls" and "Holidays" try to think of therapy activities that could use these materials. Analyze the tasks a user would perform as they used one the programs available at this site. Is the stimulation modality primarily auditory or visual? What kind of motor skills are involved in use of the program? Could the program be easily adapted for users with disabilities? Are there materials which would be of interest to children of varied cultures, age levels and gender?
4. Access one of the links that allows you to download a file. Easy, wasn't it? (NOTE: Before you download a file using your Web browser, be certain that you have identified a file on your com-

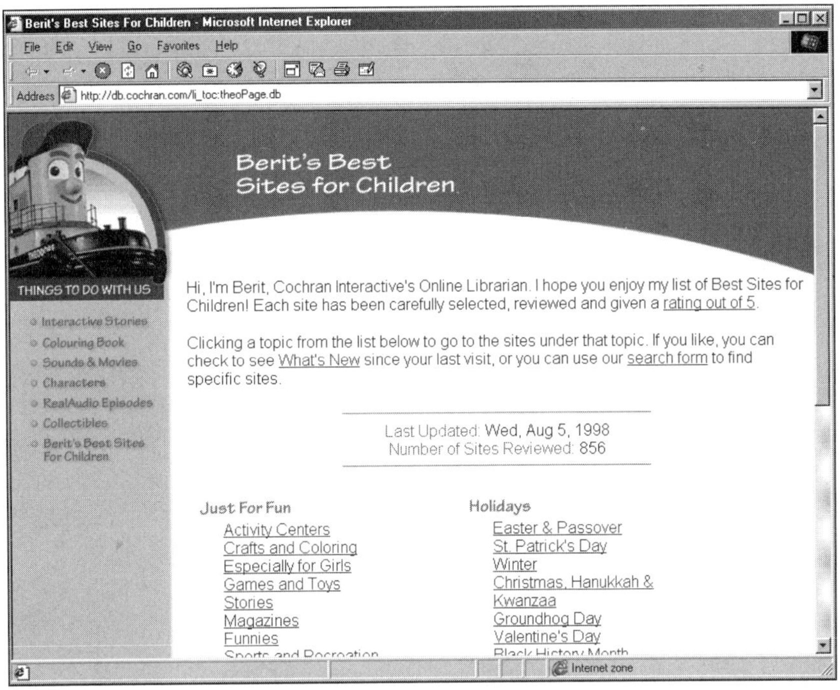

puter's hard disk in which the file can be placed. You make that choice in your browser's "Preferences" menu. You will also need a decompression program which is commonly used for your operating system—e.g., StuffIt Expander or Unzip.)

Students can also obtain software appropriate for use with adult clients, in office management tasks, and in speech analysis—low-cost shareware or freeware—by downloading files from a variety of Internet FTP sites.

1. Find some computer-delivered, multimedia materials that you can use in therapy with an adolescent or adult by searching the Web for shareware/freeware programs and downloading.
2. Go to CNET's shareware search engine <http://www.shareware.com>.
3. Use the pull-down menu at the search window to choose your operating system (e.g., Windows 95, Macintosh).
4. In the search window, type the keyword "games" or "education." You will then receive a list of programs available for downloading with descriptions, date of uploading to the site and size of the file.

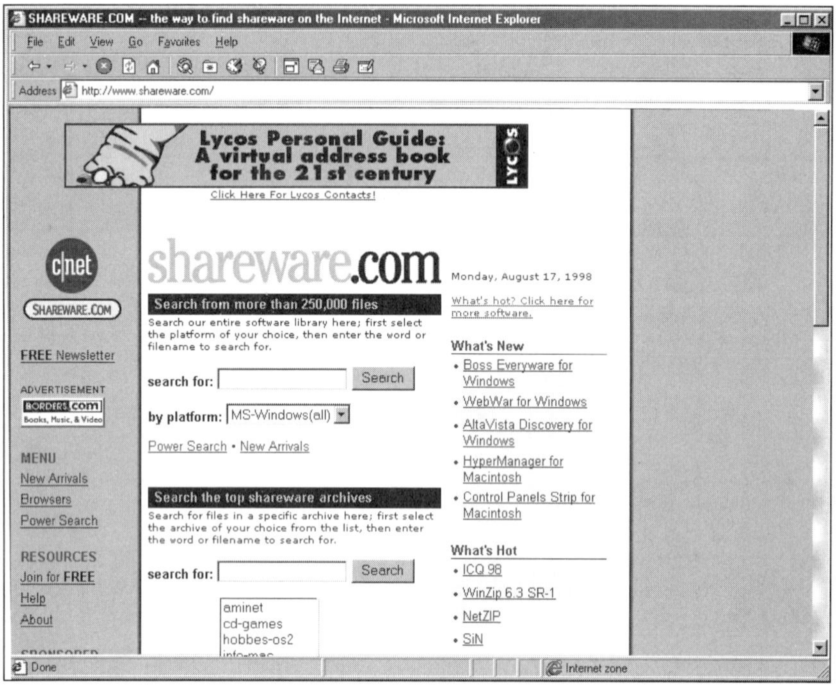

5. Click on the link for one program that appears to have some applicability for use with an adult with a language disorder and one that seems as though it might be suitable for an adolescent.

6. You will go to a page which gives you a choice of download sites rated for speed and integrity. Choose one with a four- or five-star rating. Click on that link then watch while the file is downloaded to your computer and decompressed.

7. Open the program and work through it, identifying ways of adapting it to therapy activities and goals used in treatment with persons with communication disorders.

8. You can also access FTP sites for file downloads by using a FTP client program such as Fetch or Turbogopher. Use of an FTP program is usually faster than accessing such files with a Web browser program.

Critical Evaluation

Where Seeing Is Not Always Believing

Typical research resources, such as journal articles, books, and other scholarly works, are reviewed by a panel of experts before being published. At the very least, any reputable publisher takes care to assure that the author is who he or she claims to be and that the work being published represents a reasoned and informed point of view. When anyone can post anything in a Web site or to a newsgroup, the burden of assessing the relevance and accuracy of what you read falls to you. Rumors quickly grow into facts on the Internet simply because stories can spread so rapidly that the "news" seems to be everywhere. Because the Internet leaves few tracks, in no time it's impossible to tell whether you are reading independent stories or the merely same story that's been around the world two or three times. Gathering information on the Internet may be quick, but verifying the quality of information requires a serious commitment.

Approach researching via the Internet with confidence, however, and not with trepidation. You'll find it an excellent workout for your critical evaluation skills; no matter what career you pursue, employers value an employee who can think critically and independently. Critical thinking is also the basis of problem solving, another ability highly valued by the business community. So, as you research your academic projects, be assured that you're simultaneously developing lifelong expertise.

It's Okay to Be Critical of Others

The first tip for successful researching on the Internet is to always consider your source. A Web site's URL often alerts you to the sponsor of the site. CNN or MSNBC are established news organizations, and you can give the information you find at their sites the same weight you would give to their cablecasts. Likewise, major newspapers operate Web sites with articles reprinted from their daily editions or expanded stories written expressly for the Internet. On the other hand, if you're unfamiliar with the source, treat the information the way you would any new data. Look for specifics—"66 percent of all voters" as opposed to "most voters"—and for information that can be verified—a cited report in another medium or information accessible through a Web site hosted by a credible sponsor—as opposed to generalities or unverifiable claims. Look for independent paths to the same information. This can involve careful use of search engines or visits to newsgroups with both similar and opposing viewpoints. Make sure that the "independent" information you find is truly independent. In newsgroups don't discount the possibility of multiple postings, or that a posting in one group is nothing more than a quotation from a posting in another. Ways to verify independent paths include following sources (if any) back to their origins, contacting the person posting a message and asking for clarification, or checking other media for verification.

In many cases, you can use your intuition and common sense to raise your comfort level about the soundness of the information. With both list servers and newsgroups, it's possible to lurk for a while to develop a feeling for the authors of various postings. Who seems the most authoritarian, and who seems to be "speaking" from emotion or bias? Who seems to know what he or she is talking about on a regular basis? Do these people cite their sources of information (a job or affiliation perhaps)? Do they have a history of thoughtful, insightful postings, or do their postings typically contain generalities, unjustifiable claims, or flames? On Web sites, where the information feels more anonymous, there are also clues you can use to test for authenticity. Verify who's hosting the Web site. If the host or domain name is unfamiliar to you, perhaps a search engine can help you locate more information. Measure the tone and style of the writing at the site. Does it seem consistent with the education level and knowledge base necessary to write intelligently about the subject?

When offering an unorthodox point of view, good authors supply facts, figures, and quotes to buttress their positions, expecting readers to be skeptical of their claims. Knowledgeable authors on the Internet follow these same commonsense guidelines. Be suspicious of authors who expect you to agree with their points of view simply because they've published them on the Internet. In one-on-one encounters, you frequently judge the authority and knowledge of the speaker using criteria you'd be hard pressed to explain. Use your sense of intuition on the Internet, too.

As a researcher (and as a human being), the job of critical thinking requires a combination of healthy skepticism and rabid curiosity. Newsgroups and Web sites tend to focus narrowly on single issues (newsgroups more so than Web sites). Don't expect to find a torrent of opposing views on newsgroup postings; their very nature and reason for existence dampens free-ranging discussions. A newsgroup on *The X-Files* might argue about whether extraterrestrials exist but not whether the program is the premier television show on the air today. Such a discussion would run counter to the purposes of the newsgroup and would be a violation of netiquette. Anyone posting such a message would be flamed, embarrassed, ignored, or otherwise driven away. Your research responsibilities include searching for opposing views by visiting a variety of newsgroups and Web sites. A help here is to fall back on the familiar questions of journalism: who, what, when, where, and why.

- **Who** else might speak knowledgeably on this subject? Enter that person's name into a search engine. You might be surprised to find whose work is represented on the Web. (For fun, one of the authors entered the name of a rock-and-roll New York radio disk jockey into MetaCrawler and was amazed to find several pages devoted to the DJ, including sound clips of broadcasts dating back to the sixties, along with a history of his theme song.)
- **What** event might shed more information on your topic? Is there a group or organization that represents your topic? Do they hold an annual conference? Are synopses of presentations posted on the sponsoring organization's Web site?
- **When** do events happen? Annual meetings or seasonal occurrences can help you isolate newsgroup postings of interest.
- **Where** might you find this information? If you're searching for information on wines, for example, check to see if major wine-producing regions, such as the Napa Valley in California or the Rhine Valley in Germany, sponsor Web sites. These may point you to organizations or information that don't show up in other searches. Remember, Web search engines are fallible; they don't find every site you need.
- **Why** is the information you're searching for important? The answer to this question can lead you to related fields. New drugs, for example, are important not only to victims of diseases but to drug companies and the FDA as well.

Approach assertions you read from a skeptic's point of view. See if they stand up to critical evaluation or if you're merely emotionally attached to them. Imagine "What if . . . ?" or "What about . . . ?" scenarios that may disprove or at least call into question what you're reading. Try following each assertion you pull from the Internet with the phrase, "On the other hand. . . ." Because you can't leave the sentence hanging, you'll be forced to finish it, and this will help get you into the habit of critically examining information.

These are, of course, the same techniques critical thinkers have employed for centuries, only now you are equipped with more powerful search tools than past researchers may have ever imagined. In the time it took your antecedents to formulate their questions, you can search dozens of potential information sources. You belong to the first generation of college students to enjoy both quantity and quality in its research, along with a wider perspective on issues and the ability to form personal opinions after reasoning from a much wider knowledge base. Certainly, the potential exists for the Internet to grind out a generation of intellectual robots, "thinkers" who don't think but who regurgitate information from many sources. Technology always has its good and bad aspects. However, we also have the potential to become some of the most well-informed thinkers in the history of the world, thinkers who are not only articulate but confident that their opinions have been distilled from a range of views, processed by their own personalities, beliefs, and biases. This is one of the aspects of the Internet that makes this era such an exciting combination of humanism and technology.

part 2

Internet Activities for Speech-Language Pathology and Audiology

The examples in this section are intended to stimulate further creative uses of the Internet for learning and practice in audiology and speech-language pathology. The models and exercises presented below contain Internet addresses which also appear in the Communication Disorders URLs by Content Area list. The readings as cited in this section also contain suggestions for practical application of Internet resources.

Improve Your Internet Skills

As undergraduate student in Communication Disorders, you need to maintain a high GPA by turning in outstanding papers and making impressive classroom presentations. You have previously taken one computer course in high school, used a Web browser program to find information about sports scores and you send email to your friends using Pine.

Purpose of this exercise: learn to use the Internet as effectively as possible for academic success.

Objectives:

1. learn the terminology used by others during Internet activities,
2. discover how to conduct an efficient search for information on the Internet,

3. identify relevant Communication Disorders sites that contain the most information resources.

Activity One

Read for background specific to Communication Disorders applications,

a. Shoemaker, A. (1997). Scholastic Surfing: World Wide Web Weaves Through University Classrooms. *Advance, 7(3),* 8–9.

Question: Describe one Internet resource (Web site, program, course) that you learned about by reading this article.

____

____

b. Iskowitz, M. (1997). Diving into the Internet. *Advance, 7(3),* 6–7, 46.

Question: Describe one Internet resource (Web site, program, course) that you learned about by reading this article.

____

____

Activity Two

Update your ability to understand and speak "Internetese" by going to the Web site Techencyclopedia at **<http://www.techweb.com/encyclopedia/>** for definition of over 11,000 words and concepts related to the Internet and technology, including newest terms.

Question: Define the following terms.

parental control software ______________________________

____

Web master ______________________________________

____

Active-X browser ___________________________________

____

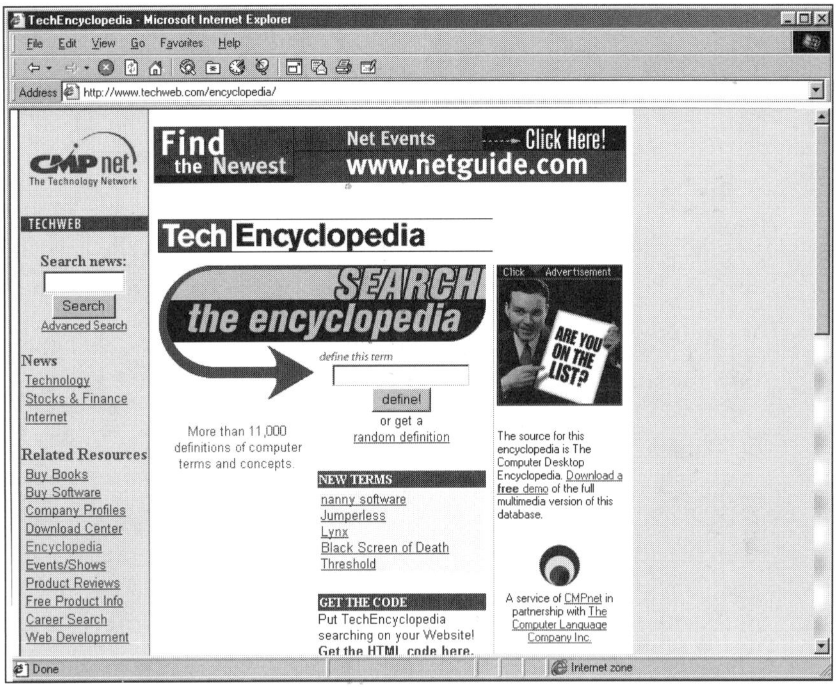

part 2

browser cache ____

____

TCP/IP ____

____

flame ____

____

netiquette ____

____

compression utility ____

____

Activity Three

Be welcome in any Internet society by improving your manners. Go to **<http://www.fau.edu/rinaldi/net/ten.html>**

Question: Which one of the ten commandments for computer ethics seemed most important to you?

____

____

Why? ____________________________________

____

You can learn some additional email manners, too. Go to **<http://www.theistudio.com/netiquette>**

Question: How do you use a discussion thread?

____

____

Question: Why is it a problem to overuse a mail distribution list?

____

____

____

Question: What do the following emoticons mean?

:-O ____________________________________

:-@ ____________________________________

:-| ____________________________________

Delivering the Goods

As an SLP graduate student, you are assigned to work with your supervisor in a middle school in which there is a population of deaf and hard of hearing students. Resource Room and Inclusion models are used to deliver the curricula to these students. Your supervisor, the school-based SLP, tells you that she wants you to develop some specific activities to use with hearing-impaired students in classroom as well as the therapy room. You are also asked to gather some informational materials to give to parents. She also wants you to help her plan and carry out an inservice program with the classroom teachers during you practicum assignment.

Purpose of exercise: To use the Internet to provide services and enhance support to the students, their teachers and families across educational settings.

Objectives:

1. devise a service delivery model tailored to the inclusive model used in the school,
2. create a therapy plan for one-to-one and small group therapy activities in pull-out and resource room settings,
3. increase internal support for students through in-service with teachers and administrators and classroom presentations for the students' peers,
4. increase external support for students by providing informational materials for families and encouraging participation in self-help groups for students/parents.

Activity One

You haven't learned anything about the inclusion model in your coursework, so you want to obtain information on SLP inclusive service delivery by going to SLP and Inclusion **<http://netnow.micron.net/~sunrise/slp.htm>**

Question: How does the SLP author of this Web site use "narratives" in an inclusion model?

Question: What adaptations would be needed to use the books recommended for use in language literacy work with children with hearing impairments?

Activity Two

Develop your therapy protocols by reviewing suggestions for aural habilitation activities at the Aural Habilitation Page **<http://ourworld.compuserve.com/homepages/srinivasan/ahpghm.htm>**

Question: Why is a stuffed toy recommended for use in improving the behavior of a deaf child?

____

____

Question: Sending hearing-impaired children on errands where they must communicate with speech is suggested as a technique for increasing the relevancy of therapy. Can you think of additional exercises to make using speech meaningful for the older deaf child?

____

____

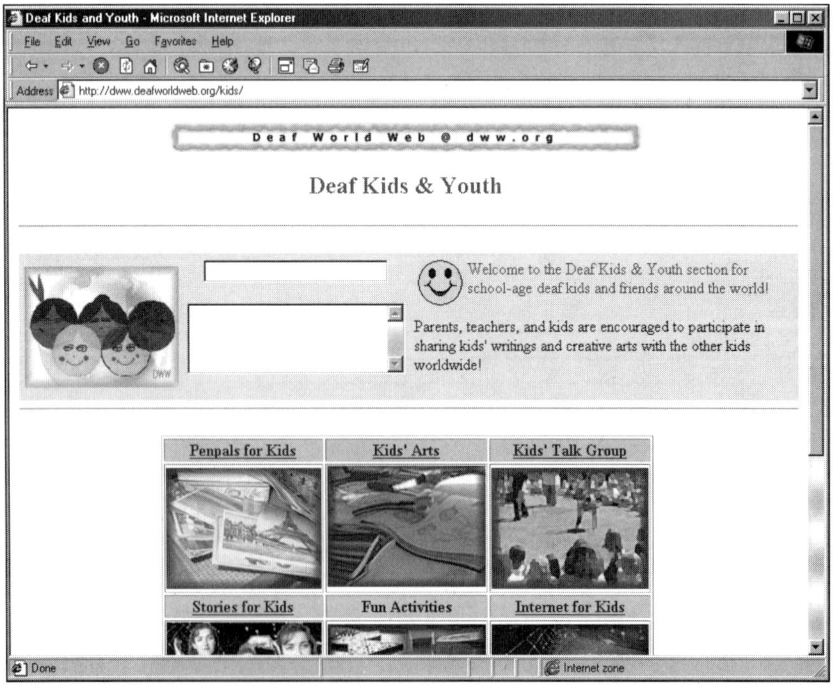

Activity Three

On a computer in the therapy room or the students' resource room, establish a subscription for students' use in an online discussion group such as Deaf Cyberkids **<http://dww.deafworldweb.org/kids/>** (younger children) or Deaf World Web **<http://dww.deafworldweb.org/>** (adolescents) and subscribe to the Newsgroup alt.support.hearing-loss on that computer's Web browser.

Question: Devise two ways you could incorporate material from these online groups into your therapy activities.

1. ____

   ____

2. ____

   ____

Activity Four

Search for Internet resources aimed at teachers of deaf and hearing-impaired children and incorporate the materials you find there into an inservice presentation which includes information on using the Web sites you find into their classroom activities.

Question: Describe a valuable site you found, list the URL and the keyword(s) you used in your search.

____

____

Question: Describe another site you found, list the URL and the keyword(s) you used in your search.

____

____

Activity Five

Devise a three-step lesson plan to use for a classroom presentation on the deaf/hearing impaired culture in classes which include any deaf or hard of hearing students. Incorporate the web site Animated American Sign Language Dictionary **<http://www.bconnex.net/~randys/>**

1. ____

   ____

2. ____

   ____

3. ____

   ____

Activity Six

Produce printouts to send home with children which contain information about hearing impairment from two consumer-oriented Web sites. Offer to demonstrate the use of these sites to parents at the next scheduled "Parents' Night" at school.

Question: Which sites did you pick and why?

____

____

Question: How could you make these sites useful for the parents who don't have access to the Internet at home or work?

____

____

Joining the Cultural Elite

You have earned your audiology degree and your first job is in a rural practice setting in which the population consists of persons of a culture(s) and language-base different from yours. You intend to acquire the skills needed to interact appropriately with your patients and develop good marketing and advocacy techniques to support your practice.

Purpose of this exercise: To provide effective service by using culture-appropriate interactions and materials.

Objectives:
1. educate self on influence of culture on service delivery,
2. obtain information specific to the culture(s) prevalent in the area,
3. review and update information on the particular types of services needed by the patient population,
4. advocate for increased services/resources for the population.

Activity One

Find at least two sections of the ASHA Web site **<http://www.asha.org>** that can help you increase your knowledge about multicultural practice.

Question: The ASHA Web site includes additional links to help you with your continuing education in this area. Describe them.

____

____

Activity Two

Search the Internet for information regarding specific cultures, checking for Web sites, discussion groups, books, journals and essays. Try to find a "jumpstation."

Question: What is a jumpstation (and whcrc did you find the definition)?

____

____

Question: List five keywords or keyphrases that were helpful to you during your search for information on different cultures.

____

____

Question: Select one of the cultures you found in your Internet search and describe three characteristics of the culture that are different than yours.

____

____

Question: List one method that you could use to accommodate tone of these differences in your practice?

____

____

Activity Three

Download informational materials for families written in their native language, such as those at Mi Pediatra **<http://www.mipediatra.com.mx/>**.

Question: List three similar sites you find by simply browsing through the multicultural Web sites you have already found.

1. ____
2. ____
3. ____

Activity Four

Find two sites through which you can contact state and federal legislators to state your concerns regarding their culturally-diverse constituency to whom you provide services.

Question: If you are uncertain as to the identity of your congress-persons, how can you find that information on the Internet?

____

____

Recommended Readings

Goldberg, B. (1997). Linking Up with Telehealth. *ASHA, Fall,* 26–31.

Iskowitz, M. (1997). Virtual clinic: Proving ground for budding audiologists. *Advance, 7(2),* 5, 42.

Kuster, J. M. (1997). Telehealth and the Internet. *ASHA, Fall,* 55.

———. (1996). Commands to remember, *ASHA, Winter,* 19.

———. (1996). More Commands to Remember. *ASHA, Spring,* 51.

Tsantis, L., Keefe D. (1996). Reinventing Education. *ASHA, Fall,* 38–41.

Communication Disorders: URLs by Content Area

Internet resources on this list are shown by the Communication Disorders Content Area to which they are most directly related. However, many of these sites are useful for several different areas of

Speech-Language Pathology and Audiology. This will become evident as you explore each resource in depth. This listing is selective, not comprehensive. Most of the sites listed here contain links to other excellent resources.

Please be aware that because the Internet is an ever-developing collection, sites frequently appear and disappear. Sometimes, the Internet address of a particular site will change. The old address will often contain a link to the new address for a limited time period—like a forwarding address at a post office. The addresses for Internet sites on this list were current at the time of publication.

Although the remainder of the content areas on this list appear in alphabetical order, the area "COMPREHENSIVE SITES" is placed first due to the significant utility of these resources. These addresses contain information-rich text and a large variety of links which are frequently updated.

Comprehensive Sites

American Academy of Audiology

`http://www.audiology.org/`

This is a wonderful site for professionals and consumers. The interface is simple. It is divided into two options: Consumers' Resources and Professionals' Resources. In both sections there are many online reprints as well as links to a large variety of sites important to audiology, hearing disorders, and deafness.

American Speech-Language-Hearing Association

`http://www.asha.org/`

This is the definitive Web site for anyone interested in Communication Disorders. The site is divided into three sections: Students, Professionals, and Consumers. The site is searchable and has an index page. A Table of Contents Service for all ASHA journals is available here. Also within the site is a Members Only section which features areas such as the Membership Directory online and searchable. The coverage of other areas within the Professionals section is almost exhaustive covering FAX-on-Demand, marketing, legislation, professional issues, continuing education, paraprofessionals, treatment outcomes, salary equivalency, classified advertisements, and so on. The Student section includes information on training programs in Communication Disorders and career and certification information. The Consumer section contains an index of ASHA brochures, some of which are online reprints, a listing of self-help groups, and basic information about choosing a speech-language pathologist or audiologist.

Berit's Best Sites for Children

http://db.cochran.com/li_toc:theoPage.db

Wow! This Web site reviews and provides links to over 800 sites with materials and activities for children. It also provides a rating for each site on a scale of 1–5. In addition, the site provides some online activities for children, including interactive stories, coloring books, and funny sounds. Many possibilities for use in therapy with children can be found here.

Deaf World Web

http://dww.deafworldweb.org/

This site has it all! Good graphics, a variety of information related to deafness, lots of links. There is information that will be valuable for children, adults, consumers and professionals here. This is the Web page on which to start your search in the areas of deafness and hearing impairment.

Internet Search Engine Forms

http://www.ama assn.org/med_link/searches.htm

This Web page, part of the American Medical Association Web site, allows the user to enter search requests to many of the top search engines from a single page. Saves time consumed by accessing multiple search pages.

Net Connections for Communication Disorders and Sciences

http://www.mankato.msus.edu/dept/comdis/kuster2/welcome.html

This site contains a mind-boggling number of links. The references are categorized by the content areas usually found in communication disorders and also professional issues. This site has become the "gold standard" for speech-language pathology and audiology internet activity and has won many awards. Its Webmaster, Judith M. Kuster, also writes the "Internet" column in ASHA magazine.

Virtual Tour of the Ear

http://ctl.augie.edu/perry/ear/ear.htm

This is the Web site of Perry Hanavan, Augustana College. Using a tabled collection of links, you are provided with a rich collection of textual and graphic information on ear anatomy, audiology, speech perception, disorders of hearing, and aural rehabilitation. It has a very attractive and well-organized graphical setup. This site also has links to several medical search engines.

Alternative/Augmentative Communication

Resource Sites

Apple K–12 Disability Resources—Shareware

http://www.apple.com/education/k12/disability/shareware.html

Contains many downloadable files (Apple/Mac compatible) for adapting computers for use by persons with disabilities.

Augmentative and Alternative Communication

http://www.asel.udel.edu/neat/aac.html

This site includes an introduction to AAC, some examples of AAC used successfully, links to AAC manufacturers and links to other Web resources.

Cerebral Palsy

http://www.irsc.org/cerebral.htm

This is an index containing many links to online information and support concerning cerebral palsy.

Closing the Gap

http://www.closingthegap.com/

Closing the Gap is an internationally recognized source for information on innovative applications of microcomputer technology in special education and rehabilitation. They publish a resource directory and newspaper. The Web site contains a research library with an annotated bibliography of articles related to many AAC topics.

Trace Research and Development Center

http://www.trace.wisc.edu/

This rehabilitative engineering research site offers search capability for textual materials on research and product at the Center. Also can search for annotated bibliography of disability documents.

United Cerebral Palsy

http://www.ucpa.org/html/

Lots of information on advocacy and disability issues with links to the latest governmental actions. Site has search capability.

Virtual Assistive Technology Center

http://www.at-center.com/

Home page gives access to lists of freeware/shareware for use in AAC.

Anatomy

Resource Sites

Airway Pathology Atlas

http://www.users.interport.net/~jsherry/airwaymap.html

Displays excellent endoscopic views of normal and abnormal vocal folds.

Anatomy of the Neck

http://www.ncl.ac.uk/~nccc/anatomy_html/

Tutorial with both text and cadaver photographs which can be enlarged. Includes quizzes on material.

Anatomy Review—Head and Neck

http://www.bcm.tmc.edu/oto/studs/anat.html

Material covers nine different head/neck structures, inluding ear, pharynx, and larynx with outlined tutorial and clear schematic graphics.

Human Anatomy Online

http://www.innerbody.com/htm/body.html

General drawings of various anatomical views. Site allows some interactivity with point and click access to textual information about anatomical structures. Good undergraduate study aid.

Marching Through the Visible Woman

http://www.crd.ge.com/cgi-bin/vw.pl

This is the distaff version of the "visible man" project and is a work in progress. Students can access information and graphics on the head and neck areas at this time. Many JPEG files are available including a Java file producing head/neck rotation, both skin and bone views.

Neuroanatomy Review

http://www.BethIsraelNY.org/inn/anatomy/anatomy.html

This WebSite from the Institute for Neurology and Neurosurgery, Beth Israel Medical Center, is meant to serve as an informational service for families of children with neurological and neurosurgical illnesses. Detailed text notes and links to colored drawings make this an excellent tutorial for undergraduate students.

Otoweb

http://www.medsch.wisc.edu/otoweb/otoweb.html

Contains animated, video, and virtual reality graphics on ear anatomy and physiology.

Visible Embryo

http://visembryo.ucsf.edu/

Display of first four weeks of embryo formation using text, microscopic photographs, and Shockwave movies (has link for downloading the Shockwave plug-in).

Visible Human Project Gallery

http://www.nlm.nih.gov/research/visible/visible_gallery.html

MRI scans of sections of a male cadaver. Articles explaining source of the project. Links to many other projects and products resulting from this work.

Vocal Tract Visualization Lab

http://som1.ab.umd.edu/~mstone/lab.html

Three-dimensional drawings of tongue surface during speech articulation.

Whole Brain Atlas

http://www.med.harvard.edu/AANLIB/home.html

Images of MRI and PET scans or normal and abnormal brains from Harvard Medical School. User can change slice location and timeline. Includes clinical profile of patients and tours of specific brain structures of interest in each patient.

Aphasia/Alzheimer's/Dementia

Discussion Groups

ALZHEIMER@WUBIOS.WUSTL.EDU
majordomo@wubios.wustl.edu

CNET_STROKE_DEM_HEAD_INJURY@LISTSERV.ARIZONA.EDU
listserv@listserv.arizona.edu

part 2

Resource Sites

Alzheimer's Association

http://www.alz.org/

Official Web site of this consumers' organization.

Alzheimer's Disease

http://www.ninds.nih.gov/healinfo/DISORDER/ALZHEIMR/alzheimers.htm

This NIDCD publication on Alzheimer's Disease includes detailed information and a current bibliography.

Aphasia Facts

http://www.nih.gov/nidcd/aphasia2.htm

Consumer information from NIDCD on aphasia, with suggestions for caregivers and reference to organizations concerned with stroke and aphasia. Links to NIH well as NIDCD home page.

National Stroke Association

http://www.stroke.org/

Information on causes and treatment for stroke. Also has quiz on Stroke Risk Factors, low cost materials ordering information, and links to other related Web sites for professionals and consumers.

Speech after Stroke

http://www.mayohealth.org/mayo/9608/htm/speech.htm

The Mayo Clinic's Health Web site offers this consumer information on speech rehabilitation following stroke.

Articulation/Motor Speech/Apraxia

Discussion Groups

APRAXIA-KIDS@AVENZA.COM
listserv@avenza.com

C-NET_UN_NEURO_DIS@LISTSERV.ARIZONA.EDU
listserv@listserv.arizona.edu

Resource Sites

Apraxia—Kids

http://www.avenza.com/~apraxia/index.html

This Web site features consumer information and articles on speech/ language evaluation and treatment, IQ testing, and an FAQ for parents. There are also links to other apraxia Web sites and a pointer for subscribing to their listserv.

Articulation Disorders FAQ

http://www.kidsource.com/ASHA/articulation.html

The KidsSource provides detailed consumer information on articulation disorders and links to related Web sites.

Developmental Verbal Dyspraxia

http://www.cs.amherst.edu/~djv/DVD.html

Gives basic information for parents and a bibliography for professionals of key articles and texts about developmental verbal dyspraxia.

Dysarthria Intelligibility Measures

http://www.ticeinfo.com/asha/asha97.html

This is an outline of the ASHA '97 presentation by Beukelman, Yorkston, and Hodge regarding their computerized measure of speech intelligibility. Contains an extensive bibliography.

Motor Speech Disorders Information

http://www.ticeinfo.com/speech/index.html

This commercial site contains large bibliographies of areas related to motor speech problems including degenerative dysarthria, developmental apraxia, and so on. Also carries links to related sites and TOC for Proceedings of Speech Motor Control Conference.

National Institute of Neurological Disorders and Stroke

`http://www.ninds.nih.gov/healinfo/nindspub.htm`

Many fact sheets and bibliographies are available at this Web site regarding neurological conditions related to motoric problems including speech functions.

Nervous System Diseases

`http://www.mic.ki.se/Diseases/c10.html`

The Karolinska Institute provides valuable links to Web sites with information regarding various aspects of neurological disease processes. Appears to be aimed primarily at the professional user.

What Is Developmental Verbal Apraxia?

`http://www.healthtouch.com/level1/leaflets/aslha/aslha032.htm`

This is an ASHA Fact Sheet provided by the HealthTouch organization Web site.

Audiology

Discussion Groups

ASHA-AUD-FORUM@POSTMAN.COM
asha-aud-forum-request@postman.com

bionet.audiology (Newsgroup)

alt.support.tinnitus (Newsgroup)

Resource Sites

Audiology Review

`http://www.bcm.tmc.edu/oto/studs/aud.html`

Tutorial on audiology in outline form accompanied by excellent schematics and audiogram graphics.

Audiologyinfo.com

http://www.audiologyinfo.com/main.shtml

This Web site has a student bulletin board, job postings, a political action connection, links to related sites, information about hearing aids, and a virtual patient presentation.

Common Diseases of the External and Middle Ear

http://www.bcm.tmc.edu/oto/studs/midear.html

Another excellent tutorial, with graphics, from Dr. Alford at Baylor College of Medicine.

Doctor C's Ear, Nose, and Throat Page

http://www.netdoor.com/entinfo/

Contains links to many of the American Academy of Otolaryngology brochures on a variety of head and neck disease problems.

Ear Infection in Children

http://www.mayohealth.org/mayo/9603/htm/otitis.htm

Good public health brochure from the Mayo Clinic. (Graphic of the ear can be enlarged online for better detail.)

Earworks

http://www.neurophys.wisc.edu/~ychen/auditory/fs-auditory.html

Complete course on auditory anatomy including animations, audiograms and microphotographic images. Easy to use interface.

Glossary of Audiology Terms

http://www.siemens-hearing.com/questions/faq/glossary.htm

The Siemens Hearing Instruments commercial site provides an online, indexed glossary of audiology terminology.

Hearing Course Text

http://www.neurophys.wisc.edu/h&b/textbook/textmain.html

Complete course on hearing and balance. Very thorough and easy to use.

Hearing Tests

http://weber.u.washington.edu/~otoweb/audiogram.html

Descriptions for consumers of basic auditory tests from the University of Washington.

An Inner Ear Primer

http://www.tmc.tulane.edu/departments/Pathology/fermin/InnerEarPrimer.html

A sophisticated tutorial on functioning of the auditory and vestibular systems of the inner ear. Includes links to detailed graphics.

Myringotomy and PE Tubes

http://www.bcm.tmc.edu/oto/clinic/educate/myring.html

Text and graphics to describe for consumers the need for and procedure of inserting ear tubes.

Otitis Media Facts

http://www.nih.gov/nidcd/otitism.htm

Another public service fact sheet from NIDCD.

Otorhinolaryngology—Basic Review Materials

http://www.bcm.tmc.edu/oto/studs/toc.html

This is the Table of Contents for a series of tutorials from the Baylor College of Medicine, Dept. of Otorhinolaryngology and Communicative Sciences.

Patient Information—American Academy of Otolaryngology—Head and Neck Surgery

http://www.entnet.org/patient.html

This site presents many consumer fact sheets, quizzes, and links to other related sites.

Virtual Audiology Patients

http://www.audiologyinfo.com/vpatient/

Case histories, test results, and audiograms for patients with hearing problems are presented here for use by practitioners and students.

Autism

Discussion Group

bit.listserv.autism (Newsgroup)

Resource Sites

Autism and Brain Development Research Laboratory

http://nodulus.extern.ucsd.edu/

Information about autism research, links to other autism sites, and links to online neuropsychology and medical journals.

Autism Fact Sheet

http://www.ninds.nih.gov/healinfo/DISORDER/AUTISM/autism.htm

Consumer fact sheet on autism from NIH.

Autism Resources

http://web.syr.edu/~jmwobus/autism/

A large index of online resource links related to autism.

Autism Society of America

http://www.unc.edu/depts/teacch/

Has information concerning educating autistic children and an online glossary of terms related to autism.

TEACCH

http://www.unc.edu/depts/teacch/

A collection of information on autism and the programs conducted under TEACCH. Good consumer and practitioner information on autism and treatment. Links to other sites on autism available here.

Child Language Disorders

Discussion Groups

CAPD@MAELSTROM.STJOHNS.EDU
listserv@maelstrom.stjohns.edu

C-PALSY@SJUVM.STJOHNS.EDU
listserv@sjuvm.stjohns.edu

C-NET_CHILDRENS_LANG_DISORDERS@LISTSERV.ARIZONA.EDU
listserv@listserv.arizona.edu

CPPARENT@SJUVM.STJOHNS.EDU
listserv@sjuvm.stjohns.edu

LANG-LEARN-ED@LISTS.WWU.EDU
listproc@lists.wwu.edu

L-HCAP@VM1.NODAK.EDU
listserv@vm1.nodak.edu

alt.support.cerebral-palsy (Newsgroup)

bit.listserv.down-syn (Newsgroup)

Resource Sites

Cerebral Palsy

http://galen.med.virginia.edu/~smb4v/tutorials/cp/cp.htm

A multimedia tutorial for parents and children with cerebral palsy.

Child Language Data Exchange System

http://poppy.psy.cmu.edu/childes/index.html

An online data base of child language transcript data. Computational tools for analysis also available at this site.

Computer Games for Children with Language Disabilities

http://www-cgi.cnn.com/HEALTH/9601/dyslexia_tech/index.html

This is a CNN news brief describing Tallal's research on computer-delivered slowed speech stimulation for children diagnosed with child language/dyslexia problems.

Computerized Profiling

http://www.cwru.edu/artsci/cosi/faculty/long/research/cp.htm

From Case Western Reserve University, a depository of language analysis files created using the computerized profiling program. Access to the downloadable program is free. Also contains many linguistics links.

Down Syndrome

http://www.irsc.org/down.htm

Index containing many Web links related to Down syndrome.

General Information about Speech and Language Disorders

http://www.kidsource.com/NICHCY/speech.html

A consumer fact sheet on communication disorders from KidsSource.

LD Resources

http://www.ldresources.com/

This site has a variety of writings concerning children with language/learning problems. It also includes downloadable software for use by practitioners, parents, and children.

Speech and Language Milestone Chart

http://www.kidsource.com/LDA/speech_language.html

This chart of developmental levels to age six years of speech and language in children was composed by the Learning Disabilities Association of America. Also contains pointers to articles on this topic.

Spoken Language Problems

http://www.kidsource.com/LDA/spoken_language.html

A consumer fact sheet from KidsSource.

Symposium on Research in Child Language Disorders

http://www.waisman.wisc.edu/srcld/

Linked abstracts for papers delivered at this conference every year since 1995.

Clefting/Craniofacial Disorders

Discussion Groups

CLEFT-TALK@MOTHER.COM
listproc@mother.com

CTTEEN@WIDESMILES.ORG
webmaster@widesmiles.org, with the notation, Subscribe CTTeen

Resource Sites

About Cleft Lip and Cleft Palate

http://www.cleft.com/cleft.htm

Fact sheet from the American Cleft Palate—Craniofacial Association.

About Face

http://www.interlog.com/~abtface/

A support and information Web site about people with facial differences.

Cleft Palate-Craniofacial Clinic at Boystown

http://www.boystown.org/chlc/cleftp.htm

There are links to other CLP Web sites on this home page and two excellent photographs of primary palate cleft repair.

Cleft Palate Repair

http://bpass.dentistry.dal.ca/cleftrepair/cleftrepair.html

Case studies of cleft repairs with online, enlargeable pre- and post-surgery photographs.

CleftNet

http://www.surgery.uiowa.edu:80/surgery/plastic/cleftnet.html

Quiz and basic information from the University of Iowa Plastic Surgery Unit.

Craniofacial Anomalies

http://cpmcnet.columbia.edu/dept/nsg/PNS/Craniofacial.html

"The topics discussed are written specifically for parents and relatives of children with conditions that require care from a neurosurgeon. As best as possible the information has been written in "plain English" and is not intended to be a reference for professionals."

Introduction to Cleft Lip and Palate

http://www.bcm.tmc.edu/oto/grand/6191.html

Presentation for professionals in a grand rounds format. Includes a bibliography.

Palatal Rehabilitation

http://www.bcm.tmc.edu/oto/grand/2493.html

Another grand rounds presentation from Baylor College of Medicine.

Pediatric—Perinatal Pathology Index

http://www-medlib.med.utah.edu/WebPath/PEDHTML/PEDIDX.html#1

Contains several good photographs of cleft lip/palate formations.

Velocardiofacial Syndrome

http://www.crosslink.net/~marchett/vcfs/vcfs.shtml

Information for professionals and parents on this problem, also known as Schprintzen Syndrome. Contains links to articles and support groups.

Widesmiles!

http://www.widesmiles.org/

This site offers many support services for parents and is an information-rich source for professionals, containing many links to bibliographies and other CLP-related sites.

Deaf/Hearing Impaired

Discussion Groups

DEAFBLND@UKCC.UKY.EDU
listserv@ukcc.uky.edu

DEAF DISCUSSION GROUPS
http://dww.deafworldweb.org/chat/

EDUDEAF@LSV.UKY.EDU
listserv@lsv.uky.edu

PARENTDEAF-HH@LIST.EDUC.KENT.EDU
listproc@list.educ.kent.edu

alt.support.hearing-loss (Newsgroup)

bit.listserv.deaf-L (Newsgroup)

Resource Sites

Animated American Sign Language Dictionary

http://www.bconnex.net/~randys/

This site provides both videos and animations demonstrating signs and fingerspelling for a glossary of English vocabulary items. Also contains many links to related sites.

Center for Hearing Loss in Children—Boystown

http://www.boystown.org/chlc/

This site contains many information fact sheets and links for both parents and professionals regarding hearing loss, hearing aids, and deafness.

Children of Deaf Adults

http://www.gallaudet.edu:80/~rgpricke/coda/

"CODA is an organization that focuses on hearing children of deaf adults. Membership is primarily, but not exclusively, composed of hearing children of deaf parents. CODA addresses our bicultural experiences through conferences, support groups, and resource development."

Deaf Cyberkids

http://dww.deafworldweb.org/kids/

This Web site is focused on children with opportunities such as particpating in a talk group, communicating with penpals, displaying their art work. There is also a link for parents, educators, and professionals to a Deaf Discussion Group.

Deaf Education Option Web

http://www2.pair.com/options/

Presented here are descriptions and discussion concerning the various communication training options that can be used by deaf children and their families. Includes information regarding technology.

Dr. Dave's Deaf and Hard of Hearing Links

http://members.aol.com/DrDaveLink/audiology.htm

Contains many links in both audiology and speech-language pathology in the U.S., Europe, and Great Britain. Lists graduate training programs for teachers of the deaf.

Gallaudet University

http://www.gallaudet.edu/

Information and application capability for undergraduate and graduate students who are deaf, hard of hearing and hearing. Also has a FAQ on deafness and online search capabilities.

Hard of Hearing and Deaf Students: A Resource Guide to Support Classroom Teachers

http://www.bced.gov.bc.ca/specialed/hearimpair/toc.htm

Contains links to a number of documents intended to educate teachers including: sample audiograms, sample questions for parents, notes for team meetings, sample questions for student interviews, communication tip sheets, classroom adaptations, equipment needs.

National Information Center on Deafness

http://www.gallaudet.edu/~nicd/

Links for professionals and consumers alike along with information sheets such as "State-wide services for deaf and hard of hearing," and "Health services for deaf and hard of hearing." Online search capability.

Listen Up & Talk It Up

http://members.tripod.com/~listenup/

Web site established by the parent of a hard of hearing child. Includes discussion of communication stimulation program marketed on the site. Many related links for both parents and children.

Self-Help for Hard of Hearing People

http://www.audiology.com/consumer/shhhfram.htm

This consumer organization presents position papers on many issues related to hearing loss. Site also has excerpts from the Shhh journal, *Hearing Loss,* and has links to many related sites.

Speechreading

http://mambo.ucsc.edu/psl/lipr.html

Contains publication abstracts and graphics from several researchers in the area of lipreading.

Strategies for Communication between the Hearing and Hearing-Impaired

http://www.weizmann.ac.il/deaf-info/comm_strategies.html

Brief outlines highlighting physical requirements for communication with persons who hear well and those who don't.

Strategies for Teaching Children with Hearing Impairments

http://www.central.edu/education/REX/hi.html

Specific lesson plans for teachers on such topics as teaching mathematics, music, sign language, and suggestions for inclusion of hard of hearing children in a regular classroom.

Tips for Therapists of Hearing Impaired Children

http://ourworld.compuserve.com/homepages/srinivasan/ahtips.htm

Yamada Web Guide to American Sign Language

http://babel.uoregon.edu/yamada/guides/asl.html

This site includes downloadable ASL fonts and links to a number of listservs related to deafness.

Fluency

Discussion Groups

STUT-HLP@ECNET.NET
listproc@ecnet.net

STUTTERING HOME PAGE CHAT ROOM
http://www.mankato.msus.edu/dept/comdis/kuster/chat/chatroom.html

STUTT-L@VM.TEMPLE.EDU
listserv@vm.templevm.edu

STUTT-X@ASUVM.INRE.ASU.EDU
listserv@asuvm.inre.asu.edu

Resource Sites

Canadian Association for People Who Stutter

http://www.webcon.net/~caps

This consumer organization Web site contains information and links for consumers and professionals alike. Some sections are presented in French as well as English. Nice Web page layout.

Cluttering Bibliography

http://www.mankato.msus.edu/dept/comdis/kuster/cluttering/clutterbib.html

An extensive bibliography on cluttering from the Net Connections site.

International Stuttering Association

http://www.xs4all.nl/~edorlow/isa.html

Presents list and links for stuttering associations and Web pages around the world. Also has a link to Scatman John's Web site.

National Stuttering Project

http://www.nspstutter.org/

This excellent Web site gives the user access to many resources without the need to pursue other stuttering links—most of which are listed at this site. Archives for the outstanding monthly newsletter Letting Go are available as well as abstracts, and often the complete text, of articles in the current issue. Information for consumers is available at this site for no cost, with a listing of other resources—videos, brochures, pamphlets, at very low cost. There are many materials available for those wishing to start a stuttering support group.

Prevention of Stuttering in Young Children

http://www.prevent-stuttering.com/Prevention.html

From Canada, information about stuttering for parents. Also includes links to sites of interest to both professionals and parents. Includes some French language information.

Stuttering

http://www.familyvillage.wisc.edu/lib_stut.htm

A fairly bare-bones site listing many resources available both off- and online.

Stuttering Facts

http://www.nih.gov/nidcd/stutter.htm

This is a NIDCD fact sheet which also lists contact points for stuttering information.

Stuttering Foundation of America

http://www.stuttersfa.org/

This site makes available the full text of many of the popular SFA brochures including four which are written in Spanish. Emphasis on prevention as well as treatment.

Treating the School Age Stutterer

http://www.mankato.msus.edu/dept/comdis/kuster/TherapyWWW/components/treatschoolage.html

Contains a complete protocol for therapy with this population.

Understanding Stuttering

http://www.msnbc.com/onair/nbc/dateline/stutter/default.asp

This Web site displays a broadcast from MSNBC on 2,500 years of stuttering.

General Resource Links

Bibliographic Formats for Citing Electronic Information

http://www.uvm.edu/~ncrane/estyles/

This Web site contains detailed information on electronic citations forms to be used in reference according to the APA and MLA formats.

Big Pages of Special Education Links

http://www.mts.net/%7Ejgreenco/special.html

There are a multitude of links to many resources for children with disabilities, their families, their teachers and their therapists.

California Virtual University

http://www.california.edu/

This is an index with links for descriptions and enrollment in courses offered by distance education and online from California's colleges and universities.

CD Courses on the Web

http://www.utexas.edu/world/lecture/comsci/

The Web site from University of Texas, Austin, contains lists not only of online CD courses, but also U.S. university Web sites and U.S. K–12 Web sites.

Geroweb Virtual Library on Aging

http://www.iog.wayne.edu/cgi-bin/ROFM.acgi

Many Web links to resources on aging.

Glossary from the Mayo Clinic

http://www.mayohealth.org/mayo/glossary/htm/index.htm

The Web site makes available a glossary of medical terms accompanied by an audio pronunciation of the terms.

A Guide for Writing Research Papers

http://webster.commnet.edu/apa/apa_intro.htm

An FAQ based on the American Psychological Association style guidelines.

Kid Health

http://kidshealth.org/index.html

The health of children is the focus of many publications, online resources and links intended for use by professionals, children, and parents.

Kidsource, Inc.

http://www.kidsource.com

Education and healthcare information is extracted from many different sources and presented at this site. Includes information on computing and software for children.

Lifelong Learning

http://www.geteducated.com/dlsites.htm

This is a directory of distance education, virtual university, and other online training sites. Contains informational materials about using Internet education opportunities.

Mayo Clinic Health Oasis

http://www.mayohealth.org/

This Web site is the online public information organ for the Mayo Clinic. Contains many online fact sheets on different health issues. Has search capabilities.

MedHelp International

http://www.medhelp.org/

There is an extensive online medical library available at this Web site as well as the latest medical news from Johns Hopkins. Has an "Ask the doctor" feature.

Medical Matrix

http://www.medmatrix.org/index.asp

This searchable site is a compendium of resources related to clinical medicine intended for medical and health-related professionals. It includes links to a variety of medical specialty sites, disease topic sites, journal indices, and so forth.

Multimedia Medical Reference Library

http://www.med-library.com/medlibrary/

Search capability of medical books, journals, references, colleges, professional organizations, and software is the strength of this Web site.

Online Etiquette

http://www.theistudio.com/netiquette

A resource which is self-described as, "Online social graces for newbies and lazy netizens."

Pediatric Points of Interest

http://www.med.jhu.edu/peds/neonatology/poi.html

Contains a myriad of links to all areas of pediatric medicine such as journal articles, medical topic-specific sites, humor and art, children's Web sites, parenting support, electronic consultations.

PubMed

http://www.ncbi.nlm.nih.gov/PubMed/

This Web site provides a FREE Medline and Pre-Medline search engine from the National Library of Medicine.

Roget's Thesaurus Search Engine

http://humanities.uchicago.edu/forms_unrest/ROGET.html

Users can complete full text searches through a public domain edition of Roget's Thesaurus here.

RXList

http://www.rxlist.com/

At this Web site, you can complete searches on a drug index by name of the drug and by keyword. Gives brand names, generic names, indications for use, dosages, side effects, and interactions.

Shareware

http://www.shareware.com/

This site is associated with the television program CNET.com. It contains several different categories of shareware sites, such as "Most Popular," "New," and so on. It will provide you with a description of the software and statistics on the posting date and size of the file, and provides a link which takes you to sites appropriate to your operating system platform for the downloading process.

Special Needs Education Network

http://www.schoolnet.ca/sne/e/snewww.html

This Web site is a product of Canada's SchoolNet. It includes links to Web information on a variety of topics. It also offers links for teacher and parent resources and a directory of 5,000 special needs organizations.

Techencyclopedia

http://www.techweb.com/encyclopedia/

Defines over 11,000 words and concepts related to the Internet and technology. Also lists newest terms.

Technology 2000

http://www.asha.org/professionals/tech_resources/tech2000/3.htm

Online ASHA report regarding clinical applications of computers and the Internet in speech-language pathology and audiology.

The Net: User Guidelines and Netiquette

http://www.fau.edu/netiquette/net/

A compendium of Internet user responsibilities and privileges in all forms of online communication.

webTeacher

http://www.webteacher.org/winnet/indextc.html

This instructional Web site offers tutorials in many aspects of Internet functions such as search strategies, downloading and uploading files, teleconferencing, and using Web browsers. In addition, there is a wealth of instruction on building and mounting your own Web page using sound and graphic files, Java scripts, and so forth.

Government/Law

National Institute of Deafness and Other Communication Disorders

http://www.nih.gov/nidcd/

NIDCD is an agency that funds research in the areas of hearing balance, taste, smell voice, speech and language functions. This Web site contains information about grants and contracts available in this area as well as descriptions of current research. However, it also contains an index to fact sheets on communication disorders, many of which are available online for downloading such as "Noise Induced Hearing Loss" and "Recent Research on Aphasia." The NIDCD Clearing House also available here contains a searchable index of publication related to deafness and communication disorders which are not indexed elsewhere.

National Institutes of Health

http://www.nih.gov/

From this Web site, you can access many national government agencies including the National Library of Medicine, all the agencies that fall under NIH, such as the National Institute of Neurological Disorders and Stroke, National Institute of Deafness and Other Communication Disorders, National Institute of Child Health and Human Development, and the National Institute on Aging. Online search is available at this site.

Occupational Safety and Health Administration (OSHA)

http://www.osha.gov/

This U.S. Department of Labor agency allows the user to access full text of many OSHA publications and standards. There is also searchable statistical data and an FAQ available. Another valuable page gives the user links to all U.S. Government Internet sites such as the White House, Library of Congress and Department of Education.

SpeciaLaw

http://www.edlaw.net/public/contents.htm

Access to rules, regulations and guidance regarding Special Education laws can be found here. The user can access statutes and policy regarding IDEA, ADA, and FERPA. IEP Interpretation guidelines are also available.

U.S. Congress on the Internet (Thomas)

http://rs9.loc.gov/home/thomas.html

At this Web site, the user can search on U.S. House and Senate bills by number or can perform a word search and can read full text of most bills. There are directories for U.S. Senators, Representatives, and Committees. It also contains information regarding current congressional actions on the floor, committee activities, access to the *Congressional Record*, and an FAQ.

Laryngectomy

Discussion Groups

LARYNX-C@listserv.acor.org
listserv@listserv.acor.org

Resource Sites

American Cancer Society

http://www.cancer.org/

Official Web site of this organization. Searchable.

Cancer of the Larynx

http://cancer.med.upenn.edu/disease/larynx/index.html

This Web site belongs to the University of Pennsylvania ONCONET. It contains discussions of medical and psychosocial issues of importance to cancer patients, families and physicians as well as links to many related sites. It provides an annotated bibliography of recent articles on laryngeal cancer. It also has two PDQs from the National Cancer Institute—one for health care providers and one for patients—which give detailed information on all stages of laryngeal cancer as well as its prevention.

Dutch Helms' Laryngectomee Site

http://members.aol.com/fantumtwo/cancer1.htm

This is a Web site from a man who's "been there, done that." Lots of good, practical information and advice available on the pages at this site, along with many links to related information.

Laryngeal Cancer (Patient)

http://www.noah.cuny.edu:8080/cancer/nci/cancernet/201519.html

This Web site provides the patient PDQ on laryngeal cancer in Spanish as well as English.

LarynxLink

http://www.larynxlink.com/

A variety of information for laryngectomees and about laryngectomy is available. A map directory of IAL support groups and another of "speech instructors" is one of the resources here, along with articles written by professionals and laryngectomees, access to the text of recent newsletters and a directory of laryngectomee suppliers.

Post-Laryngectomy Voice Restoration

http://www.inhealth.com/educationalresourcesindexpage.htm

Inhealth Technologies provides good information and online, enlargeable graphics regarding esophageal speech, artificial larynges, and tracheo-esophageal puncture.

Laryngeal Cancer: The Voice Center

http://www.voice-center.com/larynx_ca.html

Good explanations of all aspects of laryngeal cancer, including terminology and speech after laryngectomy.

Multicultural Issues

Read article:

Kuster, J. M. (1997). Multicultural/Diversity Internet Resources *ASHA, Spring,* 50.

Discussion Groups

C-NET_CULTURAL_ISSUES@LISTSERV.ARIZONA.EDU
listserv@listserv.arizona.edu

HIJOS-ESP@LISTSERV.REDIRIS.ES
listserv@listserv.rediris.es

alt.language.ebonics (Newsgroup)

Resource Sites

Children and Bilingualism

http://www.kidsource.com/asha/bilingual.html

This page at the KidsSource Web site provides another ASHA fact sheet with links to additional information about minority gifted and talented children.

Cross-Cultural and Cross-Lingual Links

http://pegasus.cc.ucf.edu/~abrice/Cross-cultural.html

As its name implies, this Web site contains an exhaustive listing of links to culturally diverse sites for conferences, journals, language testing, ethnography, research, diversity and disability, and more. A really valuable information resource.

Cultural and Linguistic Diversity

http://www.thinkingpublications.com/board/11culture.html

A list of postings on Cultural and Linguistic Diversity appears on this page of Thinking Publications Web site.

Mi Pediatra

http://www.mipediatra.com.mx/

This Web site delivers pediatric medical information for parents in Spanish. Includes a wealth of information on illnesses and other problems as well as terminology listings.

Neurological

Discussion Groups

MSLIST@TECHNION.TECHNION.AC.IL
listserv@technion.technion.ac.il

PARKINSN@LISTSERV.UTORONTO.CA
listserv@listserv.utoronto.ca

alt.support.ataxia (Newsgroup)

alt.support.mult.sclerosis (Newsgroup)

Resource Sites

Acquired Neurogenic Disorders

http://www.thinkingpublications.com/board/05neuro.html

This is the Speech-Language Pathology Bulletin Board from Thinking Publications which contains postings on neurological disorders.

Amyotrophic Lateral Sclerosis Association

http://www.alsa.org/

Official Web site of this association. Consumer-oriented.

CenterNet

http://cnet.shs.arizona.edu/cnet.html

This page of the National Center for Neurogenic Communication Disorders enables the user to subscribe to a number of listserv administered by Centernet. It includes directions on subscription and also contains archived files.

National Parkinson Foundation

http://www.parkinson.org/

Consumer-oriented information with many links and a library with many free and online publications.

Neurological Disorders in Children

http://www.BethIsraelNY.org/inn/index.html

The Institute of Neurology and Neurosurgery at Beth Israel Medical Center has provided professional-level information on several neurological conditions and general information on neuroanatomy at this site.

Neurology Web Forum

http://neuro-www.mgh.harvard.edu/forum/

At this Web site, patients and physicians can have online chats about neurological disease issues.

Speech and Multiple Sclerosis

http://aspin.asu.edu/msnews/schspee.htm

This page, sponsored by the International MS Support Foundation, discusses areas of speech, language, swallowing, and cognition which may be affected by multiple sclerosis. Self-help suggestions for working with any problems which result are also presented at this Web site.

Professional Organizations/Issues

Note: This section lists the addresses for Web site home pages of many professional organizations and issue discussions of interest to speech-language pathologists and audiologists.

Read articles:

Kuster, J. M. (1996). Organization Home Pages. *ASHA, Fall,* 42.

———. (1997). Ethics and the Internet. *ASHA, Winter, 33.*

———. (1998). Job Hunting Online. *ASHA, Winter,* 33.

Discussion Groups

ASHA Members' Discussion Forums

http://www.asha.org/Asha_Member/forum.htm

Resource Sites

Acoustical Society of America

http://asa.aip.org/

American Academy of Private Practice in Speech Pathology and Audiology

http://www.aappspa.org/

American Cleft Palate-Craniofacial Association

http://www.cleft.com/

American Medical Association

http://www.ama-assn.org/sitemap.htm

American Psychological Association

http://www.apa.org/

Canadian Association of Speech-Language Pathologists and Audiologists

http://www.caslpa.ca/

Council for Exceptional Children

http://www.cec.sped.org/

Council of Graduate Programs in Communication Sciences and Disorders

http://www.cgpcsd.org/

Educational Audiology Association

http://pip.ehhs.cmich.edu/eaa/

International Association for the Study of Child Language

http://atila-www.uia.ac.be/IASCL/Inhoud.html

Rehabilitation Engineering and Assistive Technology Society of North America

http://www.resna.org/

RehabJobs

http://www.rehabjobs.com/
Presents job information and advertisements for rehabilitation therapists in the fields of speech-language pathology, audiology, physical therapy,

and occupational therapy. Also contains links to other rehabilitation Web sites and limited discussion forums.

Publications—Table of Contents/Abstracts Review

Note: This section lists the address for access to a Table of Contents service for a number of journals of interest to speech-language pathologists and audiologists. Often, abstracts of articles in the journals are also available.

Access for All ASHA Journals

http://www.asha.org/professionals/publications/publications.htm

Archives of Otolaryngology—Head and Neck Surgery

http://www.ama-assn.org/public/journals/otol/otolhome.htm

Archives of Pediatrics and Adolescent Medicine

http://www.ama-assn.org/public/journals/ajdc/ajdchome.htm

Brain and Development

http://www.elsevier.nl/inca/publications/store/5/2/4/1/7/2/

Child Development Abstracts and Bibliographies

http://www.journals.uchicago.edu/CDAB/journal/cdab.html

Clinical Linguistics & Phonetics Journal

http://www.tandfdc.com/JNLS/CLP.HTM

Hearsay (Journal from University of Georgia)

http://www.coe.uga.edu/csdclinic/Newsletter/news.html

Journal of the Acoustical Society of America

http://sound.media.mit.edu/~dpwe/AUDITORY/jasa/

Journal of the American Medical Association

http://www.ama-assn.org/public/journals/jama/
jamahome.htm

Journal of Children's Communication Disorders

http://pegasus.cc.ucf.edu/~abrice/jccd.html

Journal of Communication Disorders

http://www.elsevier.nl:80/inca/publications/store/
5/0/5/7/6/8/

Journal of the Experimental Analysis of Behavior

http://ehsct7.envmed.rochester.edu/wwwrap/behavior/
jeab/jeabindx.htm

Journal of Experimental Psychology: Learning, Memory, and Cognition

http://www.apa.org/journals/xlm/599tc.html

Journal of Fluency Disorders

http://www.elsevier.nl:80/inca/publications/store/
5/0/5/7/7/1/index.htt

New England Journal of Medicine—Online

http://www.nejm.org/content/index.asp

Neuropsychologia

http://www.elsevier.nl/inca/publications/store/2/4/7/

Otolaryngology—Head and Neck Surgery

http://www1.mosby.com/Mosby/Periodicals/Medical/
OHNS/hn.html

Research in Developmental Disabilities

http://www.elsevier.nl/inca/publications/store/8/2/6/

Technology and Disability

http://www.elsevier.nl/inca/publications/store/5/2/5/0/2/3/

Speech and Hearing Science

Bell Laboratories

http://www.bell-labs.com/

Bell Labs is a leader in speech science applied research. Information relevant to Communication Disorders at this site includes a library of books and IEEE proceedings, a musuem, archived science photos, and online demonstrations of text-to-speech synthesis.

comp.speech FAQ

http://svr-www.eng.cam.ac.uk/comp.speech/index.html

This site in England is a section of the comp.speech FAQ covering many aspects of speech science knowledge and research activities. Also contains many links to speech technology Web sites around the world.

Expressive Synthesized Speech

http://cahn.www.media.mit.edu/people/cahn/emot-speech.html

This Web page at the M.I.T. Media Laboratory has online examples of synthesized speech samples which were developed as part of a master's thesis.

Haskins Laboratories

http://www.haskins.yale.edu/haskins/inside.html

This is the Web site of Haskins Laboratories at Yale University. Leaders in the field of speech research such as Cooper, Liberman, and Studdert-

Kennedy have done much of their work at this lab. Information at this site includes descriptions of current speech/language research with online links to the principle researchers, a description of the Labs' history—also the history of much significant research in speech, and many links to related sites.

Institute of Phonetics

http://fonsg3.let.uva.nl/Reading_Room.html

This page of the Institute's Web site includes links to many areas of speech science including phonetics, speech perception, and linguistics, links to journals in these areas, and to several online dictionaries related to these topics.

Museum of Speech Analysis and Synthesis

http://mambo.ucsc.edu/psl/smus/smus.html

This museum resides at the Web site of the UCSC Perceptual Science Laboratory. The museum page contains information, diagrams and photographs, historical instrumentation, and researchers in speech science.

Speech on the Web

http://www.tue.nl/ipo/hearing/webspeak.htm

This Web site is described as a "jumpstation for speech synthesis." It contains many links related to the study of phonetics, both human and synthesized speech.

Speech Processing and Auditory Perception Laboratory—UCLA

http://www.icsl.ucla.edu/~spapl/

This Web site presents descriptions of current speech perception and speech production research at the lab including demonstrations of speech, diagrams, MRI images, and CV samples.

Speech Visualization Tutorial

http://lethe.leeds.ac.uk/research/cogn/speech/tutorial/index.html

Contained here is a demonstration tutorial on reading waveforms and spectrographic output. It contains graphics including a 3-D spectrogram and human speech sounds.

Ucsc Perceptual Science Laboratory

http://mambo.ucsc.edu/

This Web site has a very nice facial animation on the home page! It contains online abstracts and links for speech perception by ear as well as lipreading and facial animation. It also contains a Gopher index on PsychInfo and online book reviews in the American Journal of Psychology.

Swallowing

Discussion Groups

C-NET_SWALLOWING_DISORDERS@LISTSERV.ARIZONA.EDU
listserv@listserv.arizona.edu

DYSPHAGIA@CYBERPORT.COM
listserv@listserv.cyberport.com

Resource Sites

Dysphagia Resource Center

http://www.dysphagia.com/index.htm

Tutorials, reviews, article abstracts, anatomical images, and case studies all related to dysphagia and GERD can be found at this Web site.

Feeding Issues

http://pwp.ibl.bm/~mitchell/feeding.htm

This is one page in a Web site on cerebral palsy. This page contains a description of feeding issues in this population and presents some "common-sense" solutions. The text is written by an OT and a SLP.

Swallowing Disorders

http://www.netdoor.com/entinfo/swallaao.html

This Web site contains a comprehensive fact sheet on swallowing from the American Academy of Otolaryngology–Head and Neck Surgery.

Ultrasound Swallowing Study

http://www.cc.nih.gov/rm/sp/normal.html

This page from the NIH Web site contains a 1.7 mB Quicktime movie of an ultrasound image of a normal swallow.

Traumatic Brain Injury

Discussion Groups

TBI-SPRT@MAELSTROM.STJOHNS.EDU
listserv@maelstrom.stjohns.edu

bit.listserv.tbi-support (Newsgroup)

Resource Sites

Brain Injury Ring

http://www.webring.org/cgi-bin/webring?ring=bir;list

This Web site is a valuable resource for professionals and consumers. It contains informational pages, chat rooms, and links to other sites. It addresses pediatric, kids, and teens with both serious and fun links and activities that could be used for treatment purposes. Be sure to check this one.

Head Injury Tutorial

http://www.BethIsraelNY.org/inn/headinju/hdinj_id.html

This Web page contains information on classification and treatment for head injuries.

Traumatic Brain Injury Gopher

gopher://gopher.sasquatch.com/

This is a pointer to Gopher indices on head injury. Lots of information here.

Traumatic Brain Injury Survival Guide

http://www.tbiguide.com/

This is an online publication by Dr. Glen Johnson, Clinical Director of the Neuro-Recovery Head Injury Program in Michigan.

Treatment Resources

Note: The Internet sites listed in this section present both commercial and non-commercial information on materials, techniques, and instrumentation that can be used in therapy with persons with communication disorders.

Read article:

Crane, R. (1997). Adapting Shareware to the Clinic. *Advance, 7(3)*, 10.

Resource Sites

Botulinum Toxin Treatment

http://isis.nlm.nih.gov/nih/cdc/www/83txt.html

Canyonlands Publishing, Inc.

http://canyonlandsaz.com/

Casa Futura Technologies

http://www.casafuturatech.com/

Communication Disorders Technology, Inc.

http://www.comdistec.com/products.html

Computer Assisted Treatment Resources

http://www.mankato.msus.edu/dept/comdis/kuster2/software.html

Computer Learning Foundation

http://www.computerlearning.org/Index.htm

Contains many interesting links for children in an age-graded area called "A Safe Well-Lighted Place." Good links for educators as well.

Early Language Intervention

http://www.audiospeech.ubc.ca/eli/elimenu.htm

Educational and Therapy Games

http://www.parentpals.com/4.0Teaching/teaching.html

English as a Second Language

http://www.aci.on.ca/lighthouse/esl.html

Hanen Center

http://www.hanen.org/

How to Get the Most Out of Stuttering Therapy

http://www.mankato.msus.edu/dept/comdis/kuster/TherapyWWW/Profitingfromtherapy.html

Kay Elemetrics Corp.

http://www.kayelemetrics.com/

Kids Web

http://www.npac.syr.edu/textbook/kidsweb/

Macintosh Disability Freeware and Shareware

http://www.ECNet.Net/users/gnorris/place.shtml

Parrot Software

http://www.parrotsoftware.com/

Siemens Consumers' Corner

http://www.siemens-hearing.com/consumer/consumer%20corner.htm

SLPs and Inclusion

http://netnow.micron.net/~sunrise/slp.htm

Thinking Publications, Inc.

http://www.thinkingpublications.com/

Tice Information Pages

http://www.ticeinfo.com/index.html

Tracheoesophageal Voice Prostheses

http://www.inhealth.com/featuredproductindex.htm

Windows Software for People with Disabilities

http://www.at-center.com/windows.html

Voice

Discussion Groups

SID3VOICE@PMSYS.WEEG.UIOWA.EDU
mxserver@pmsys.weeg.uiowa.edu

Resource Sites

Atlanta Voice and Swallowing Center

http://www.mindspring.com/~newvoice/

This Center's Web site has informational fact sheets on vocal hygiene, voice problems, voice science and vocal fold microsurgery. Contains some nice photographs of the vocal folds.

Analysis by Synthesis of Severely Pathological Voices

`http://www.icsl.ucla.edu/~spapl/projects/pathological.html`

This Web site presents article abstracts and demonstration files of natural and synthesized disordered voices.

Center for Voice Disorders

`http://www.bgsm.edu/voice/`

At this Web site, there are valuable information sheets with extensive bibliographies on reflux and voice disorders, vocal nodules and polyps, singers, spasmodic dysphonia, and laryngeal disease. In addition, there is a "gallery" of very clear, color photographs of vocal folds in different pathological conditions.

GERD Information Resource Center

`http://www.gerd.com/`

"Here you will find educational resources on Gastroesophageal Reflux Disease ("GERD") for the general public, health care providers, and researchers alike. This site is intended to answer your most 'burning' questions about GERD in an educational way."

National Center for Voice and Speech

`http://www2.shc.uiowa.edu/ncvs_home.html`

This Web site at the University of Iowa contains FAQs and online reprints on vocal hygiene and links to other sites related to voice.

Spasmodic Dysphonia FAQ

`http://www.nih.gov:80/nidcd/spasdysp.htm`

A fact sheet from NIDCD is located here. It contains information describing spasmodic dysphonia, its etiology, diagnosis, and treament options.

University of Pittsburgh Voice Center

http://www.upmc.edu/upmcvoice/default.htm

There are many nice photographs at this Web site as well as information on all aspects of voice disorders, diagnosis, and treatment using a Voice Team approach.

Vocal Cord Paralysis

http://www.utmb.edu/oto/Grnds.dir/vocalparal.htm

A very thorough tutorial for professionals on vocal cord function and paralysis.

Voice Center at Eastern Virginia Medical School

http://www.voice-center.com/index.html

There is lots of content at this site. It contains text, drawings, and photographs related to laryngeal anatomy, vocal fold structure and physiology, laryngeal examination, instrumentation, spectrograms, voice disorders, and other laryngeal disorders, and an index to other areas of otolaryngology. The drawings and diagrams are excellent.

Voice Grand Rounds

http://www.bcm.tmc.edu/oto/grand/laryngology.html

The Baylor College of Medicine's Grand Rounds Archives–Laryngology Web site contains information, case presentations, and bibliographies on a number of different vocal pathologies.

Voice Institute of West Texas

http://www.acu.edu/academics/voiceinstitute/home.html

At this Web site, the user will find good demonstration materials consisting of text, photographs, and sounds related to voice production.

Wilbur James Gould Voice Research Center

http://web1.dcpa.org/wilbur_home.html

This Web site presents information on care of the voice and treatment of voice disorders.

Documentation

Your Citation for Exemplary Research

There's another detail left for us to handle—the formal citing of electronic sources in academic papers. The very factor that makes research on the Internet exciting is the same factor that makes referencing these sources challenging: their dynamic nature. A journal article exists, either in print or on microfilm, virtually forever. A document on the Internet can come, go, and change without warning. Because the purpose of citing sources is to allow another scholar to retrace your argument, a good citation allows a reader to obtain information from your primary sources, to the extent possible. This means you need to include not only information on when a source was posted on the Internet (if available) but also when you obtained the information.

The two arbiters of form for academic and scholarly writing are the Modern Language Association (MLA) and the American Psychological Association (APA); both organizations have established styles for citing electronic publications.

MLA Style

In the fifth edition of the *MLA Handbook for Writers of Research Papers,* the MLA recommends the following formats:

- **URLs:** URLs are enclosed in angle brackets (<>) and contain the access mode identifier, the formal name for such indicators as "http" or "ftp." If a URL must be split across two lines, break it only after a slash (/). Never introduce a hyphen at the end of the first line. The URL should include all the parts necessary to identify uniquely the file/document being cited.

  `<http://www.csun.edu/~rtvfdept/home/index.html>`

- **An online scholarly project or reference database:** A complete online reference contains the title of the project or database (underlined); the name of the editor of the project or database (if given);

electronic publication information, including version number (if relevant and if not part of the title), date of electronic publication or latest update, and name of any sponsoring institution or organization; date of access; and electronic address.

The Perseus Project. Ed. Gregory R. Crane. Mar. 1997. Department of Classics, Tufts University. 15 June 1998 <http://www.perseus.tufts.edu/>.

If you cannot find some of the information, then include the information that is available. The MLA also recommends that you print or download electronic documents, freezing them in time for future reference.

- **A document within a scholarly project or reference database:** It is much more common to use only a portion of a scholarly project or database. To cite an essay, poem, or other short work, begin this citation with the name of the author and the title of the work (in quotation marks). Then, include all the information used when citing a complete online scholarly project or reference database, however, make sure you use the URL of the specific work and not the address of the general site.

Cuthberg, Lori. "Moonwalk: Earthlings' Finest Hour." Discovery Channel Online. 1999. Discovery Channel. 25 Nov. 1999 <http://www.discovery.com/indep/newsfeatures/moonwa lk/challenge.html>.

- **A professional or personal site:** Include the name of the person creating the site (reversed), followed by a period, the title of the site (underlined), or, if there is no title, a description such as Home page (such a description is neither placed in quotes nor underlined). Then, specify the name of any school, organization, or other institution affiliated with the site and follow it with your date of access and the URL of the page.

O'Connor, Tom. Megalinks in Criminal Justice. North Carolina Wesleyan College. 4 Jan. 2000 <http://faculty.ncwc.edu/toconnor/>.

Some electronic references are truly unique to the online domain. These include email, newsgroup postings, MUDs (multiuser domains) or MOOs (multiuser domains, object-oriented), and IRCs (Internet Relay Chats).

Email In citing email messages, begin with the writer's name (reversed) followed by a period, then the title of the message (if any) in quotations as it appears in the subject line. Next comes a description of the message, typically "Email to," and the recipient (e.g., "the author"), and finally the date of the message.

Davis, Jeffrey. "Web Writing Resources." Email to Nora Davis. 3 Jan. 2000.

Sommers, Laurice. "Re: College Admissions Practices." Email to the author. 12 Dec. 1999.

List Servers and Newsgroups In citing these references, begin with the author's name (reversed) followed by a period. Next include the title of the document (in quotes) from the subject line, followed by the words "Online posting" (not in quotes). Follow this with the date of posting. For list servers, include the date of access, the name of the list (if known), and the online address of the list's moderator or administrator. For newsgroups, follow "Online posting" with the date of posting, the date of access, and the name of the newsgroup, prefixed with news: and enclosed in angle brackets.

Applebaum, Dale. "Educational Variables." Online posting. 29 Jan. 1998. Higher Education Discussion Group. 30 January 1993 <jlucidoj@unc.edu>.

Gostl, Jack. "Re: Mr. Levitan." Online posting. 13 June 1997. 20 June 1997 <news:alt.edu.bronxscience>.

MUDs, MOOs, and IRCs Citations for these online sources take the form of the name of the speaker(s) followed by a period. Then comes the description and date of the event, the forum in which the communication took place, the date of access, and the online address prefixed by "telnet//".

Guest. Personal interview. 24 December 1999. LinguaMOO. 24 December 1999 <telnet://du.edu:8888>.

For more information on MLA documentation style, check out their Web site at http://www.mla.org/set_stl.htm

APA Style

The *Publication Manual of the American Psychological Association* (4th ed.) is fairly dated in its handling of online sources, having been published before the rise of the WWW and the generally recognized format for URLs. The format that follows is based on the APA manual, with modifications proposed by Russ Dewey <www.psychwww.com/resource/apacrib.htm>. It's important to remember that, unlike the MLA, the APA does not include temporary or transient sources (e.g., letters, phone calls, etc.) in its "References" page, preferring to handle them in in-text citations exclusively. This rule holds for electronic sources as well: email, MOOs/MUDs, list server postings, etc., are not included in the "References" page, merely cited in text, for example, "But Wilson has rescinded his earlier support for these policies" (Charles Wilson, personal email to the author, 20 November 1996). But also note that many list server and Usenet groups and MOOs actually archive their correspondences, so that there is a permanent site (usually a Gopher or FTP server) where those documents reside. In that case, you would want to find the archive and cite it as an unchanging source. Strictly speaking, according to the APA manual, a file from an FTP site should be referenced as follows:


```
Deutsch, P. (1991). "Archie-An electronic directory
   service for the Internet" [Online]. Available
   FTP: ftp.sura.net Directory: pub/archie/docs
   File: whatis.archie.
```

However, the increasing familiarity of Net users with the convention of a URL makes the prose description of how to find a file <"Available FTP: ftp.sura.net Directory: pub/archie/docs File: whatis.archie"> unnecessary. Simply specifying the URL should be enough.

So, with such a modification of the APA format, citations from the standard Internet sources would appear as follows.

FTP (File Transfer Protocol) Sites To cite files available for downloading via FTP, give the author's name (if known), the publication date (if available and if different from the date accessed), the full title of the paper (capitalizing only the first word and proper nouns), the address of the FTP site along with the full path necessary to access the file, and the date of access.

Deutsch, P. (1991) "Archie-An electronic directory service for the Internet." [Online]. Available: ftp://ftp.sura.net/pub/archie/docs/whatis.archie.

WWW Sites (World Wide Web) To cite files available for viewing or downloading via the World Wide Web, give the author's name (if known), the year of publication (if known and if different from the date accessed), the full title of the article, and the title of the complete work (if applicable) in italics. Include any additional information (such as versions, editions, or revisions) in parentheses immediately following the title. Include the full URL (the http address) and the date of visit.

Burka, L. P. (1993). A hypertext history of multi-user dungeons. MUDdex. http://www.utopia.com/talent/lpb/muddex/essay/ (13 Jan. 1997).

Tilton, J. (1995). Composing good HTML (Vers. 2.0.6). http://www.cs.cmu.edu/~tilt/cgh/ (1 Dec. 1996).

Telnet Sites List the author's name or alias (if known), the date of publication (if available and if different from the date accessed), the title of the article, the title of the full work (if applicable) or the name of the Telnet site in italics, and the complete Telnet address, followed by a comma and directions to access the publication (if applicable). Last, give the date of visit in parentheses.

Dava (#472). (1995, 3 November). A deadline. *General (#554). Internet Public Library. telnet://ipl.sils.umich.edu:8888, @peek 25 on #554 (9 Aug. 1996).

Help. Internet public library. telnet://ipl.org:8888/, help (1 Dec. 1996).

Synchronous Communications (MOOs, MUDs, IRC, etc.) Give the name of the speaker(s), the complete date of the conversation being referenced in parentheses (if different from the date accessed), and the title of the session (if applicable). Next, list the title of the site in italics, the protocol and address (if applicable), and any directions necessary to access the work. If there is additional information such as archive addresses or file numbers (if applicable), list the word "Available," a colon, and the archival information. Last, list the date of access, enclosed in parentheses. Personal interviews do not need to be listed in the References, but do need to be included in parenthetic references in the text (see the APA *Publication Manual*).

Basic IRC commands. irc undernet.org, /help (13 Jan. 1996).

Cross, J. (1996, February 27). Netoric's Tuesday cafe: Why use MUDs in the writing classroom? MediaMoo. telenet://purple-crayon.media.mit.edu: 8888, @go Tuesday. Available: ftp://daedalus.com/ pub/ACW/NETORIC/catalog.96a (tc 022796.log). (1 Mar. 1996).

part 2

Gopher Sites List the author's name (if applicable), the year of publication (if known and if different from the date accessed), the title of the file or paper, and the title of the complete work (if applicable). Include any print publication information (if available) followed by the protocol (i.e., gopher://) and the path necessary to access the file. List the date that the file was accessed in parentheses immediately following the path.

Massachusetts Higher Education Coordinating Council. (1994) [Online]. Using coordination and collaboration to address change. Available: gopher://gopher.mass.edu:170/00gopher_root%3A%5B_hecc%5D_plan.

Email, Listservs, and Newsgroups Give the author's name (if known), the date of the correspondence in parentheses (if known and if different from the date accessed), the subject line from the posting, and the name of the list (if known) in italics. Next, list the address of the listserv or newsgroup. Include any archival information after the address, listing the word "Available" and a colon and the protocol and address of the archive. Last, give the date accessed enclosed in parentheses. Do not include personal email in the list of References. See the APA *Publication Manual* for information on in-text citations.

Bruckman, A. S. MOOSE crossing proposal. mediamoo@media.mit.edu (20 Dec. 1994).

Heilke, J. (1996, May 3). Re: Webfolios. acw-l@ttacs.
ttu.edu. Available: http://www.ttu.edu/lists/acw-l/
9605 (31 Dec. 1996).

Laws, R. UMI thesis publication. alt.education.
distance (3 Jan. 1996).

Other authors and educators have proposed similar extensions to the APA style, too. You can find URLs to these pages at

`www.psychwww.com/resource/apacrib.htm`

and

`www.nouveaux.com/guides.htm`

Another frequently-referenced set of extensions is available at

`www.uvm.edu/~ncrane/estyles/apa.htm`

Remember, "frequently-referenced" does not equate to "correct" or even "desirable." Check with your professor to see if your course or school has a preference for an extended APA style.

appendix

A URL Index for Speech-Language Pathology and Audiology

About Cleft Lip and Cleft Palate
http://www.cleft.com/cleft.htm

About Face
http://www.interlog.com/~abtface/

Access to Table of Contents for All ASHA Journals
http://www.asha.org/professionals/publications/publications.htm

Acoustical Society of America
http://asa.aip.org/

Acquired Neurogenic Disorders
http://www.thinkingpublications.com/board/05neuro.html

Airway Pathology Atlas
http://www.users.interport.net/~jsherry/airwaymap.html

Alzheimer's Association
http://www.alz.org/

Alzheimer's Disease
http://www.ninds.nih.gov/healinfo/DISORDER/ALZHEIMR/alzheimers.htm

American Academy of Audiology
http://www.audiology.org/

American Academy of Private Practice in Speech Pathology and Audiology
http://www.aappspa.org

appendix

A

American Cancer Society
http://www.cancer.org/

American Cleft Palate-Craniofacial Association
http://www.cleft.com/

American Medical Association
http://www.ama-assn.org/sitemap.htm

American Psychological Association
http://www.apa.org/

American Speech-Language-Hearing Association
http://www.asha.org/

Amyotrophic Lateral Sclerosis Association
http://www.alsa.org/

Analysis By Synthesis of Severely Pathological Voices
http://www.icsl.ucla.edu/~spapl/projects/pathological.html

Anatomy of the Neck
http://www.ncl.ac.uk/~nccc/anatomy_html/

Anatomy Review—Head and Neck
http://www.bcm.tmc.edu/oto/studs/anat.html

Animated American Sign Language Dictionary
http://www.bconnex.net/~randys/

Aphasia Facts
http://www.nih.gov/nidcd/aphasia2.htm

Apple K-12 Disability Resources—Shareware
http://www.apple.com/education/k12/disability/shareware.html

Apraxia—Kids
http://www.avenza.com/~apraxia/index.html

Archives of Otolaryngology—Head and Neck Surgery
http://www.ama-assn.org/public/journals/otol/otolhome.htm

Archives of Pediatric and Adolescent Medicine
http://www.ama-assn.org/public/journals/ajdc/ajdchome.htm

Articulation Disorders Faq
http://www.kidsource.com/ASHA/articulation.html

Asha Members' Discussion Forums
http://www.asha.org/Asha_Member/forum.htm

Atlanta Voice and Swallowing Center
http://www.mindspring.com/~newvoice/

Audiologyinfo.com
http://www.audiologyinfo.com/main.shtml

Audiology Review
http://www.bcm.tmc.edu/oto/studs/aud.html

Augmentative and Alternative Communication
http://www.asel.udel.edu/neat/aac.html

Autism and Brain Development Research Laboratory
http://nodulus.extern.ucsd.edu/

Autism Fact Sheet
http://www.ninds.nih.gov/healinfo/DISORDER/AUTISM/autism.htm

Autism Resources
http://web.syr.edu/~jmwobus/autism/

Autism Society of America
http://www.unc.edu/depts/teacch/

Bell Laboratories
http://www.bell-labs.com/

Berit's Best Sites for Children
http://db.cochran.com/li_toc:theoPage.db

Bibliographic Formats for Citing Electronic Information
http://www.uvm.edu/~ncrane/estyles/

Big Pages of Special Education Links
http://www.mts.net/%7Ejgreenco/special.html

Botulinum Toxin Treatment
http://isis.nlm.nih.gov/nih/cdc/www/83txt.html

Brain and Development
http://www.elsevier.nl/inca/publications/store/5/2/4/1/7/2/

Brain Injury Ring
http://www.webring.org/cgi-bin/webring?ring=bir;list

California Virtual University
http://www.california.edu/

Canadian Association for People Who Stutter
http://www.webcon.net/~caps

appendix
A

Canadian Association of Speech-Language Pathologists and Audiologists
http://www.caslpa.ca/

Cancer of the Larynx
http://cancer.med.upenn.edu/disease/larynx/index.html

Canyonlands Publishing, Inc.
http://canyonlandsaz.com/

Casa Futura Technologies
http://www.casafuturatech.com/

CD Courses on the Web
http://www.utexas.edu/world/lecture/comsci/

CenterNet
http://cnet.shs.arizona.edu/cnet.html

Center for Hearing Loss in Children—Boystown
http://www.boystown.org/chlc/

Center for Voice Disorders
http://www.bgsm.edu/voice/

Cerebral Palsy
http://galen.med.virginia.edu/~smb4v/tutorials/cp/cp.htm

Cerebral Palsy
http://www.irsc.org/cerebral.htm

Child Development Abstracts and Bibliographies
http://www.journals.uchicago.edu/CDAB/journal/cdab.html

Child Language Data Exchange System
http://poppy.psy.cmu.edu/childes/index.html

Children and Bilingualism
http://www.kidsource.com/asha/bilingual.html

Children's Language Disorders
http://w3.arizona.edu/~cnet/cld.html

Children of Deaf Adults
http://www.gallaudet.edu:80/~rgpricke/coda/

CleftNet
http://www.surgery.uiowa.edu:80/surgery/plastic/cleftnet.html

Cleft Palate-Craniofacial Clinic at Boystown
http://www.boystown.org/chlc/cleftp.htm

Cleft Palate Repair
http://bpass.dentistry.dal.ca/cleftrepair/cleftrepair.html

Clinical Linguistics & Phonetics Journal
http://www.tandfdc.com/JNLS/CLP.HTM

Closing the Gap
http://www.closingthegap.com/

Cluttering Bibliography
http://www.mankato.msus.edu/dept/comdis/kuster/cluttering/clutterbib.html

Common Diseases of the External and Middle Ear
http://www.bcm.tmc.edu/oto/studs/midear.html

Communication Disorders Technology, Inc.
http://www.comdistec.com/products.html

comp.speech FAQ
http://svr-www.eng.cam.ac.uk/comp.speech/index.html

Computer-Assisted Treatment Resources
http://www.mankato.msus.edu/dept/comdis/kuster2/software.html

Computer Games for Children with Language Disabilities
http://www-cgi.cnn.com/HEALTH/9601/dyslexia_tech/index.html

Computer Learning Foundation
http://www.computerlearning.org/Index.htm

Computerized Profiling
http://www.cwru.edu/artsci/cosi/faculty/long/research/cp.htm

Council for Exceptional Children
http://www.cec.sped.org/

Council of Graduate Programs in Communication Sciences and Disorders
http://www.cgpcsd.org/

Craniofacial Anomalies
http://cpmcnet.columbia.edu/dept/nsg/PNS/Craniofacial.html

Cross-Cultural and Cross-Lingual Links
http://pegasus.cc.ucf.edu/~abrice/Cross-cultural.html

Cultural and Linguistic Diversity
http://www.thinkingpublications.com/board/11culture.html

Cultural Issues
http://w3.arizona.edu/~cnet/ci.html

Deaf Cyberkids
http://dww.deafworldweb.org/kids/

Deaf Discussion Groups
http://dww.deafworldweb.org/chat/

Deaf Education Option Web
http://www2.pair.com/options/

Deaf World Web
http://dww.deafworldweb.org/

Developmental Verbal Dyspraxia
http://www.cs.amherst.edu/~djv/DVD.html

Doctor C's Ear, Nose, and Throat Page
http://www.netdoor.com/entinfo/

Down Syndrome
http://www.irsc.org/down.htm

Dr. Dave's Deaf and Hard of Hearing Links
http://members.aol.com/DrDaveLink/audiology.htm

Dutch Helms' Laryngectomee Site
http://members.aol.com/fantumtwo/cancer1.htm

Dysarthria Intelligibility Measures
http://www.ticeinfo.com/asha/asha97.html

Dysphagia Resource Center
http://www.dysphagia.com/index.htm

Ear Infection in Children
http://www.mayohealth.org/mayo/9603/htm/otitis.htm

Earworks
http://www.neurophys.wisc.edu/~ychen/auditory/fs-auditory.html

Early Language Intervention
http://www.audiospeech.ubc.ca/eli/elimenu.htm

Educational and Therapy Games
http://www.parentpals.com/4.0Teaching/teaching.html

Educational Audiology Association
http://pip.ehhs.cmich.edu/eaa/

English as a Second Language
http://www.aci.on.ca/lighthouse/esl.html

Expressive Synthesized Speech
http://cahn.www.media.mit.edu/people/cahn/emot-speech.html

Feeding Issues
http://pwp.ibl.bm/~mitchell/feeding.htm

Gallaudet University
http://www.gallaudet.edu/

General Information about Speech and Language Disorders
http://www.kidsource.com/NICHCY/speech.html

Gerd Information Resource Center
http://www.gerd.com/

Geroweb Virtual Library on Aging
http://www.iog.wayne.edu/cgi-bin/ROFM.acgi

Glossary from the Mayo Clinic
http://www.mayohealth.org/mayo/glossary/htm/index.htm

Glossary of Audiology Terms
http://www.siemens-hearing.com/questions/faq/glossary.htm

A Guide for Writing Research Papers
http://webster.commnet.edu/apa/apa_index.htm

Hanen Center
http://www.hanen.org

Hard of Hearing and Deaf Students: A Resource Guide to Support Classroom Teachers
http://www.bced.gov.bc.ca/specialed/hearimpair/tod.htm

Haskins Laboratories
http://www.haskins.yale.edu/haskins/inside.html

Head Injury Tutorial
http://www.BethIsraelNY.org/inn/headinju/hdinj_id.html

Hearing Course Text
http://www.neurophys.wisc.edu/h&b/textbook/textmain.html

Hearing Tests
http://weber.u.washington.edu/~otoweb/audiogram.html

Hearsay (J. from Univ. of Georgia)
http://www.coe.uga.edu/csdclinic/Newsletter/news.html

How to Get the Most Out of Stuttering Therapy
http://www.mankato.msus.edu/dept/comdis/kuster/TherapyWWW/Profitingfromtherapy.html

Human Anatomy Online
http://www.innerbody.com/htm/body.html

An Inner Ear Primer
http://www.tmc.tulane.edu/departments/Pathology/fermin/InnerEarPrimer.html

Institute of Phonetics
http://fonsg3.let.uva.nl/Welcome.html

International Association for the Study of Child Language
http://atila-www.uia.ac.be/IASCL/Inhoud.html

International Stuttering Association
http://www.xs4all.nl/~edorlow/isa.html

Internet Search Engine Forms
http://www.ama-assn.org/med_link/searches.htm

Introduction to Cleft Lip and Palate
http://www.bcm.tmc.edu/oto/grand/6191.html

Journal of the Acoustical Society of America
http://sound.media.mit.edu/~dpwe/AUDITORY/jasa/

Journal of the American Medical Association
http://www.ama-assn.org/public/journals/jama/jamahome.htm

Journal of Children's Communication Disorders
http://pegasus.cc.ucf.edu/~abrice/jccd.html

Journal of Communication Disorders
http://www.elsevier.nl:80/inca/publications/store/5/0/5/7/6/8/

Journal of the Experimental Analysis of Behavior
http://ehsct7.envmed.rochester.edu/wwwrap/behavior/jeab/jeabindx.htm

Journal of Experimental Psychology: Learning, Memory, and Cognition
http://www.apa.org/journals/xlm/599tc.html

Journal of Fluency Disorders
http://www.elsevier.nl:80/inca/publications/store/5/0/5/7/7/1/index.htt

Kay Elemetrics Corp.
http://www.kayelemetrics.com/

Kid Health.org
http://kidshealth.org/index.html

Kidsource, Inc.
http://www.kidsource.com

Kids Web
http://www.npac.syr.edu/textbook/kidsweb/

Laryngeal Cancer (Patient)
http://www.noah.cuny.edu:8080/cancer/nci/cancernet/201519.html

LarynxLink
http://www.larynxlink.com/

LD Resources
http://www.ldresources.com/

Lifelong Learning
http://www.geteducated.com/dlsites.htm

Listen Up & Talk It Up
http://members.tripod.com/~listenup/

Macintosh Disability Freeware and Shareware
http://www.ECNet.Net/users/gnorris/place.shtml

Marching Through the Visible Woman
http://www.crd.ge.com/cgi-bin/vw.pl

Mayo Clinic Health Oasis
http://www.mayohealth.org/

Medhelp International
http://www.medhelp.org/

Medical Matrix
http://www.medmatrix.org/index.asp

Mi Pediatra
http://www.mipediatra.com.mx/

Motor Speech Disorders Information
http://www.ticeinfo.com/speech/index.html

Multimedia Medical Reference Library
http://www.med-library.com/medlibrary/

Museum of Speech Analysis and Synthesis
http://mambo.ucsc.edu/psl/smus/smus.html

Myringotomy and PE Tubes
http://www.bcm.tmc.edu/oto/clinic/educate/myring.html

National Center for Voice and Speech
http://www2.shc.uiowa.edu/ncvs_home.html

National Information Center on Deafness
http://www.gallaudet.edu/~nicd/

National Institute of Deafness and Other Communication Disorders
http://www.nih.gov/nidcd/

National Institutes of Health
http://www.nih.gov/

National Institute of Neurological Disorders and Stroke
http://www.ninds.nih.gov/healinfo/nindspub.htm

National Parkinson Foundation
http://www.parkinson.org/

National Stroke Association
http://www.stroke.org/

National Stuttering Project
http://www.mspstutter.org/

Nervous System Diseases
http://www.mic.ki.se/Diseases/c10.html

Net Connections for Communication Disorders and Sciences
http://www.mankato.msus.edu/dept/comdis/kuster2/welcome.html

New England Journal of Medicine—Online
http://www.nejm.org/content/index.asp

Neuroanatomy Review
http://www.BethIsraelNY.org/inn/anatomy/anatomy.html

Neurological Disorders in Children
http://www.BethIsraelNY.org/inn/index.html

Neurology Web Forum
http://neuro-www.mgh.harvard.edu/forum/

Neuropsychologia
http://www.elsevier.nl/inca/publications/store/2/4/7/

Occupational Safety and Health Administration (OSHA)
http://www.osha.gov/

Online Etiquette
http://www.theistudio.com/netiquette

Otitis Media Facts
http://www.nih.gov/nidcd/otitism.htm

Otolaryngology—Head and Neck Surgery
http://www1.mosby.com/Mosby/Periodicals/Medical/OHNS/hn.html

Otorhinolaryngology—Basic Review Materials
http://www.bcm.tmc.edu/oto/studs/toc.html

Otoweb
http://sadr.biostat.wisc.edu/otoweb/otoweb.html

Palatal Rehabilitation
http://www.bcm.tmc.edu/oto/grand/2493.html

Parrot Software
http://www.parrotsoftware.com/

Patient Information—American Academy of Otolaryngology—Head and Neck Surgery
http://www.entnet.org/patient.html

Pediatric—Perinatal Pathology Index
http://www-medlib.med.utah.edu/WebPath/PEDHTML/PEDIDX.html#1

Pediatric Points of Interest
http://www.med.jhu.edu/peds/neonatology/poi.html

Post-Laryngectomy Voice Restoration
http://www.inhealth.com/educationalresourcesindexpage.htm

Prevention of Stuttering in Young Children
http://www.prevent-stuttering.com/Prevention.html

PubMed
http://www.ncbi.nlm.nih.gov/PubMed/

Rehabilitation Engineering and Assistive Technology Society of North America
http://www.resna.org/

Rehabjobs
http://www.rehabjobs.com/

Research in Developmental Disabilities
http://www.elsevier.nl/inca/publications/store/8/2/6/

Roget's Thesaurus Search Engine
http://humanities.uchicago.edu/forms_unrest/ROGET.html

RXList
http://www.rxlist.com/

Self-Help for Hard of Hearing People
http://www.audiology.com/consumer/shhhfram.htm

Shareware.com
http://www.shareware.com/

Siemens Consumers' Corner
http://www.siemens-hearing.com/consumer/consumer%20corner.htm

SLPs and Inclusion
http://netnow.micron.net/~sunrise/slp.htm

Spasmodic Dysphonia FAQ
http://www.nih.gov:80/nidcd/spasdysp.htm

Specialaw
http://www.edlaw.net/public/contents.htm

Special Needs Education Network
http://www.schoolnet.ca/sne/e/snewww.html

Speechreading
http://mambo.ucsc.edu/psl/lipr.html

Speech after Stroke
http://www.mayohealth.org/mayo/9608/htm/speech.htm

Speech and Language Milestone Chart
http://www.kidsource.com/LDA/speech_language.html

Speech and Multiple Sclerosis
http://aspin.asu.edu/msnews/schspee.htm

Speech on the Web
http://www.tue.nl/ipo/hearing/webspeak.htm

Speech Processing and Auditory Perception Laboratory—UCLA
http://www.icsl.ucla.edu/~spapl/

Speech Visualization Tutorial
http://lethe.leeds.ac.uk/research/cogn/speech/tutorial/index.html

Spoken Language Problems
http://www.kidsource.com/LDA/spoken_language.html

Strategies for Communication Between the Hearing and Hearing-Impaired
http://www.weizmann.ac.il/deaf-info/comm_strategies.html

Strategies for Teaching Children with Hearing Impairments
http://www.central.edu/education/REX/hi.html

Stroke, Dementia, and Head Injury
http://w3.arizona.edu/~cnet/sdh.html

Stuttering
http://www.familyvillage.wisc.edu/lib_stut.htm

Stuttering Facts
http://www.nih.gov/nidcd/stutter.htm

Stuttering Foundation of America
http://www.stuttersfa.org/

Stuttering Home Page Chat Room
http://www.mankato.msus.edu/dept/comdis/kuster/chat/chatroom.html

Swallowing Disorders
http://www.netdoor.com/entinfo/swallaao.html

Swallowing Disorders
http://w3.arizona.edu/~cnet/sd.html

Symposium on Research in Child Language Disorders
http://www.waisman.wisc.edu/srcld/

Teacch
http://www.unc.edu/depts/teacch/

Techencyclopedia
http://www.techweb.com/encyclopedia

Technology 2000
http://www.asha.org/professionals/tech_resources/tech2000/3.htm

Technology and Disability
http://www.elsevier.nl/inca/publications/store/5/2/5/0/2/3/

The Net: User Guidelines and Netiquette
http://www.fau.edu/netiquette/net/

Thinking Publications, Inc.
http://www.thinkingpublications.com/

Tice Information Pages
http://www.ticeinfo.com/index.html

Tips for Therapists of Hearing Impaired Children
http://ourworld.compuserve.com/homepages/srinivasan/ahtips.htm

Trace Research and Development Center
http://www.trace.wisc.edu/

Tracheoesophageal Voice Prostheses
http://www.inhealth.com/featureproductindex.htm

Traumatic Brain Injury Gopher
gopher://gopher.sasquatch.com/

Treating the School Age Stutterer
http://www.mankato.msus.edu/dept/comdis/kuster/TherapyWWW/components/treatschoolage.html

Ucsc Perceptual Science Laboratory
http://mambo.ucsc.edu/

Ultrasound Swallowing Study
http://www.cc.nih.gov/rm/sp/normal.html

Understanding Stuttering
http://www.msnbc.com/onair/nbc/dateline/stutter/default.asp

United Cerebral Palsy
http://www.ucpa.org/html/

University of Pittsburgh Voice Center
http://www.upmc.edu/upmcvoice/default.htm

U.S. Congress on the Internet (Thomas)
http://rs9.loc.gov/home/thomas.html

Velocardiofacial Syndrome
http://www.crosslink.net/~marchett/vcfs/vcfs.shtml

Virtual Assistive Technology Center
http://www.at-center.com/

Virtual Audiology Patients
http://www.audiologyinfo.com/vpatient/

Virtual Tour of the Ear
http://ctl.augie.edu/perry/ear/ear.htm

Visible Embryo
http://visembryo.ucsf.edu/

Visible Human Project Gallery
http://www.nlm.nih.gov/research/visible/visible_gallery.html

Vocal Cord Paralysis
http://www.utmb.edu/oto/Grnds.dir/vocalparal.htm

Vocal Tract Visualization Lab
http://som1.ab.umd.edu/~mstone/lab.html

Voice Center at Eastern Virginia Medical School
http://www.voice-center.com/index.html

Voice Grand Rounds
http://www.bcm.tmc.edu/oto/grand/laryngology.html

Voice Institute of West Texas
http://www.acu.edu/academics/voiceinstitute/home.html

Voice Special Interest Division (Asha)
sid3voice@pmvax.weeg.uiowa.edu

webTeacher
http://www.webteacher.org/winnet/indextc.html

What Is Developmental Verbal Apraxia?
http://www.healthtouch.com/level1/leaflets/aslha/aslha032.htm

Whole Brain Atlas
http://www.med.harvard.edu/AANLIB/home.html

Widesmiles!
http://www.widesmiles.org/

Wilbur James Gould Voice Research Center
http://web1.dcpa.org/wilbur_home.html

Windows Software for People with Disabilities
http://www.at-center.com/windows.html

Yamada Web Guide to American Sign Language
http://babel.uoregon.edu/yamada/guides/asl.html

Glossary

Your Own Private Glossary

The Glossary in this book contains reference terms you'll find useful as you get started on the Internet. After a while, however, you'll find yourself running across abbreviations, acronyms, and buzzwords whose definitions will make more sense to you once you're no longer a novice (or "newbie"). That's the time to build a glossary of your own. For now, the 2DNet Webopædia gives you a place to start.

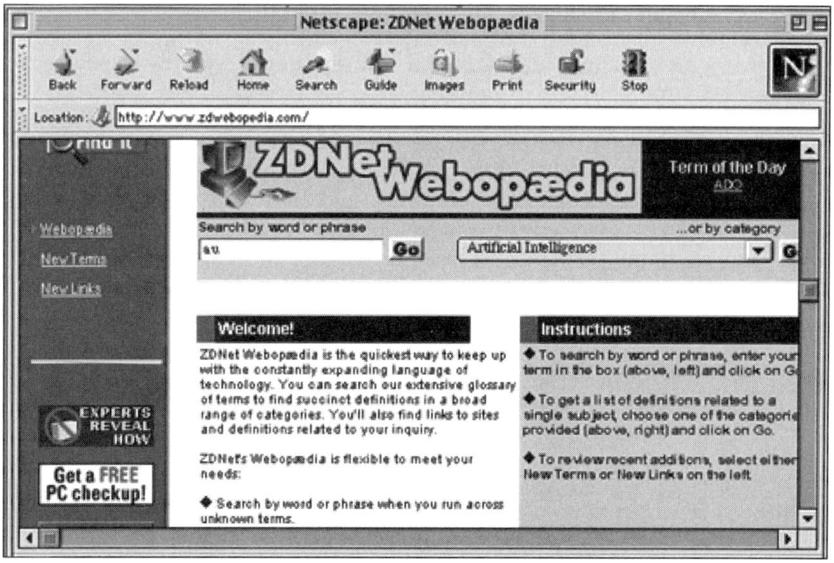

alias
A simple email address that can be used in place of a more complex one.

AVI
Audio Video Interleave. A video compression standard developed for use with Microsoft Windows. Video clips on the World Wide Web are usually available in both AVI and QuickTime formats.

bandwidth
Internet parlance for capacity to carry or transfer information such as email and Web pages.

BBS
Bulletin Board System. A dial-up computer service that allows users to post messages and download files. Some BBSs are connected to and provide access to the Internet, but many are self-contained.

browser
The computer program that lets you view the contents of Web sites.

client
A program that runs on your personal computer and supplies you with Internet services, such as getting your mail.

cyberspace
The whole universe of information that is available from computer networks. The term was coined by science fiction writer William Gibson in his novel *Neuromancer,* published in 1984.

DNS
See **domain name server.**

domain
A group of computers administered as a single unit, typically belonging to a single organization such as a university or corporation.

domain name
A name that identifies one or more computers belonging to a single domain. For example, "apple.com".

domain name server
A computer that converts domain names into the numeric addresses used on the Internet.

download
Copying a file from another computer to your computer over the Internet.

email
Electronic mail.

emoticon
A guide to the writer's feelings, represented by typed characters, such as the Smiley :-). Helps readers understand the emotions underlying a written message.

FAQ
Frequently Asked Questions

flame
A rude or derogatory message directed as a personal attack against an individual or group.

flame war
An exchange of flames (see above).

FTP
File Transfer Protocol, a method of moving files from one computer to another over the Internet.

home page
A page on the World Wide Web that acts as a starting point for information about a person or organization.

hypertext
Text that contains embedded *links* to other pages of text. Hypertext enables the reader to navigate between pages of related information by following links in the text.

LAN:
Local Area Network. A computer network that is located in a concentrated area, such as offices within a building.

link
A reference to a location on the Web that is embedded in the text of the Web page. Links are usually highlighted with a different color or underline to make them easily visible.

list server
Strictly speaking, a computer program that administers electronic mailing lists, but also used to denote such lists or discussion groups, as in "the writer's list server."

lurker
A passive reader of an Internet *newsgroup*. A lurker reads messages, but does not participate in the discussion by posting or responding to messages.

mailing list
A subject-specific automated e-mail system. Users subscribe and receive e-mail from other users about the subject of the list.

modem
A device for connecting two computers over a telephone line.

newbie
A new user of the Internet.

newsgroup
A discussion forum in which all participants can read all messages and public replies between the participants.

pages
All the text, graphics, pictures, and so forth, denoted by a single URL beginning with the identifier "http://".

plug-in
A third-party software program that will lend a web browser (Netscape, Internet Explorer, etc.) additional features.

quoted
Text in an email message or newsgroup posting that has been set off by the use of vertical bars or > characters in the left-hand margin.

search engine
A computer program that will locate Web sites or files based on specified criteria.

secure
A Web page whose contents are encrypted when sending or receiving information.

server
A computer program that moves information on request, such as a Web server that sends pages to your browser.

Smiley
See **emoticon.**

snail mail
Mail sent the old fashioned way: Write a letter, put it in an envelope, stick on a stamp, and drop it in the mailbox.

spam
Spam is to the Internet as unsolicited junk mail is to the postal system.

URL
Uniform Resource Locator: The notation for specifying addresses on the World Wide Web (e.g. http://www.abacon.com or ftp://ftp.abacon.com).

Usenet
The section of the Internet devoted to *newsgroups.*

Web browser
A program used to navigate and access information on the World Wide Web. Web browsers convert html coding into a display of pictures, sound, and words.

Web site
A collection of World Wide Web pages, usually consisting of a home page and several other linked pages.